- Learning to read starts with sounds, and phonics makes this journey simple and fun.
- In this book, children will explore long and short vowels, blending letters, and spelling rules, with silent letters shown in gray for easy recognition.
- The activities are clear and engaging to help learners build confidence step by step.
- At the end, a Certificate of Completion rewards their effort and celebrates their success.
- Be on the lookout for Book 2.

TABLE OF CONTENTS

02 — Long sound Āā – Ff
Āā, Ăă, Ȧȧ, Mm, Ss & Ff

22 — Rr – Long sound Ḡḡ
Rr, Ēē, Ĕĕ, Bb, Nn & Ḡḡ

40 — Short sound Ğğ – Dd
Ğğ, Tt, Pp, Īī, Ĭĭ & Dd

63 — Hh – Short sound C̄c̄
Hh, Ōō, Ŏŏ, Ll, Kk & C̄c̄

92 — Short sound Čč – Vv
Čč, Jj, Ww, Ūū, Ŭŭ & Vv

115 — Qq – Zz
Qq, Xx, Ȳȳ, Y̌y̌ & Zz

131 — Certificate of Completion

Trace.

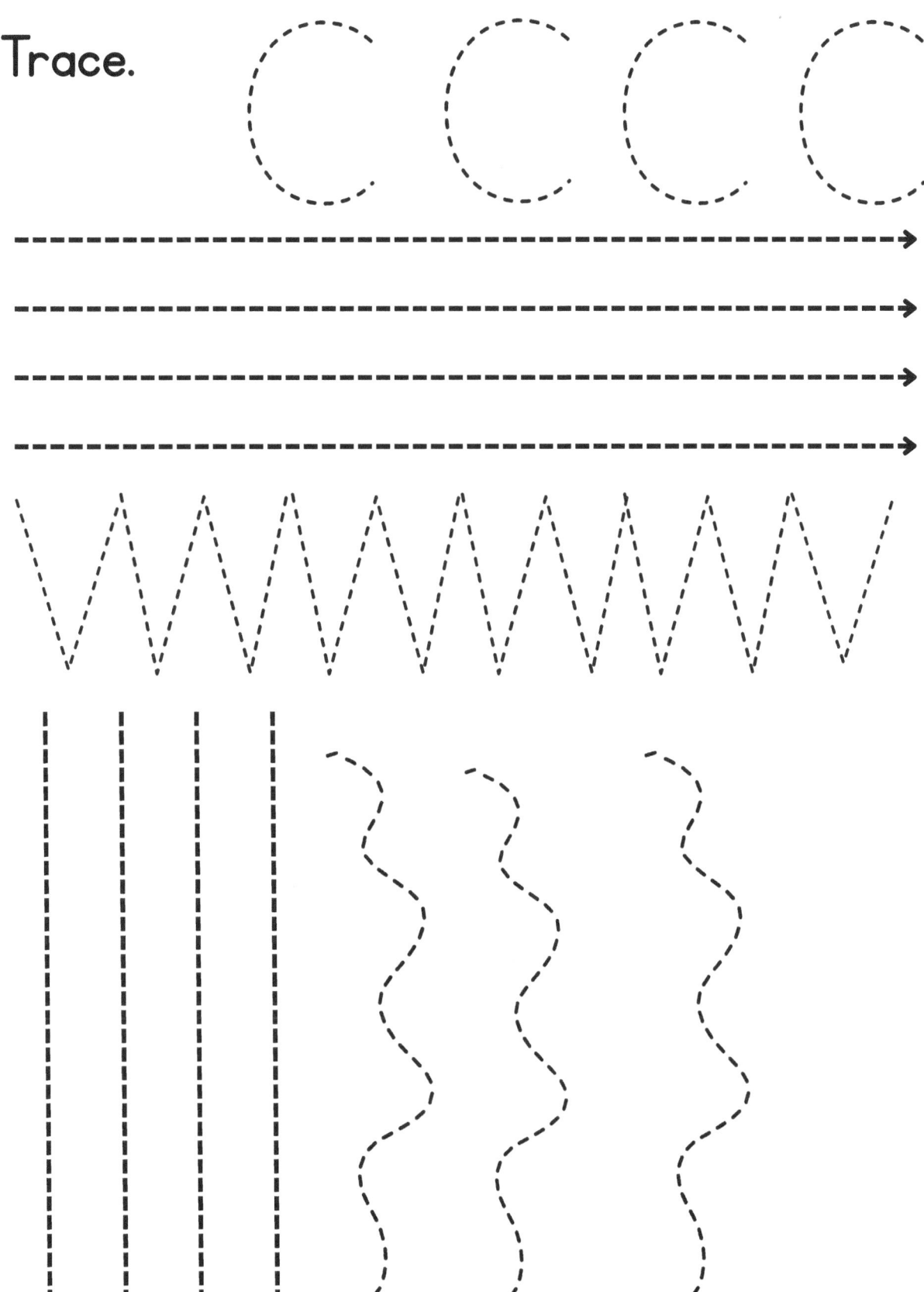

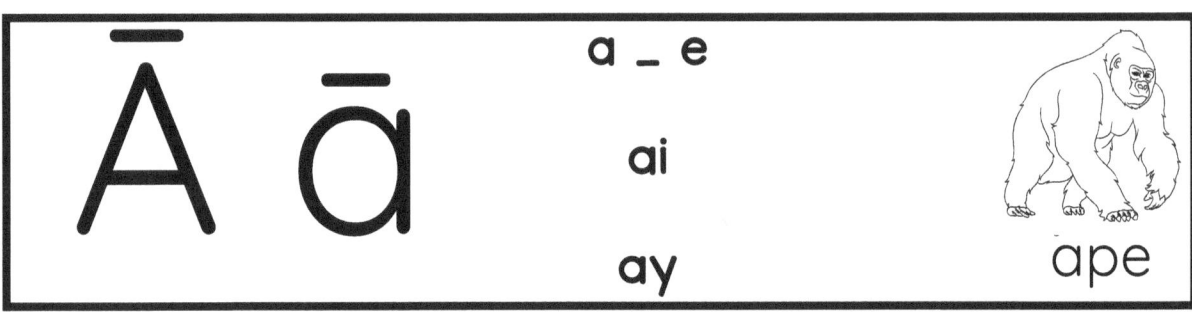

Trace the letters.

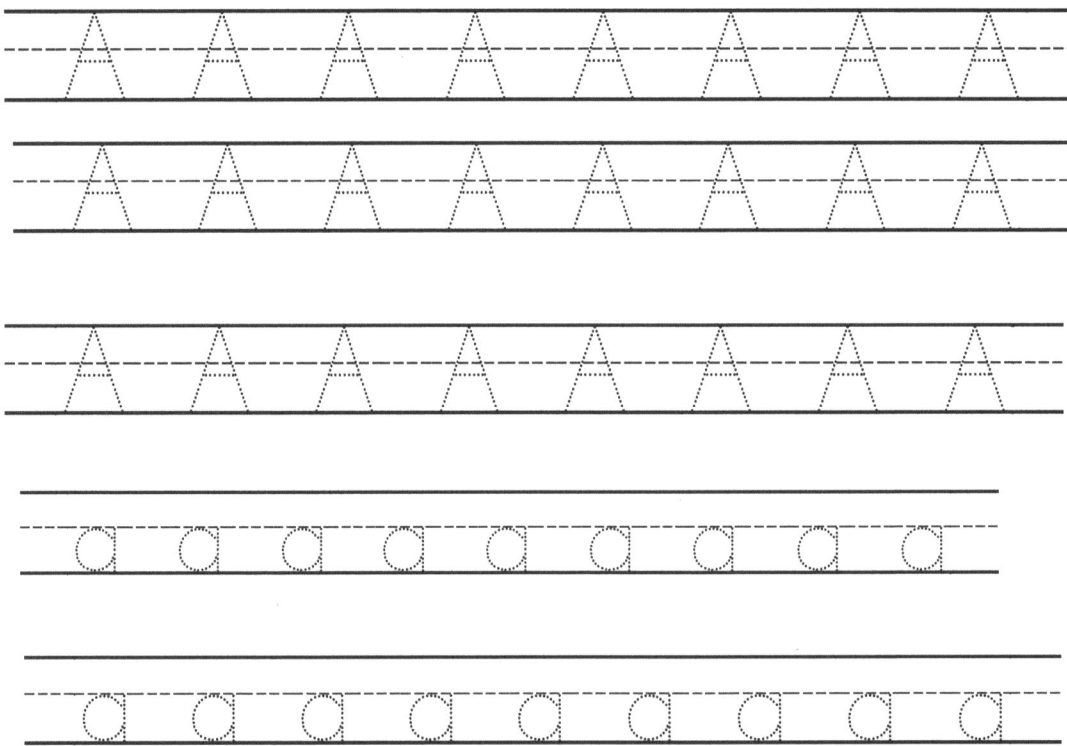

Circle A
B k A h a j N e R
A M x A f z C g A
b a s v l A F a c r

Circle a
B k p h a j N e R
A M x A f z C g a
b a s v l a F a c r

Color 4 pictures with the Āā sound in blue.

Trace.

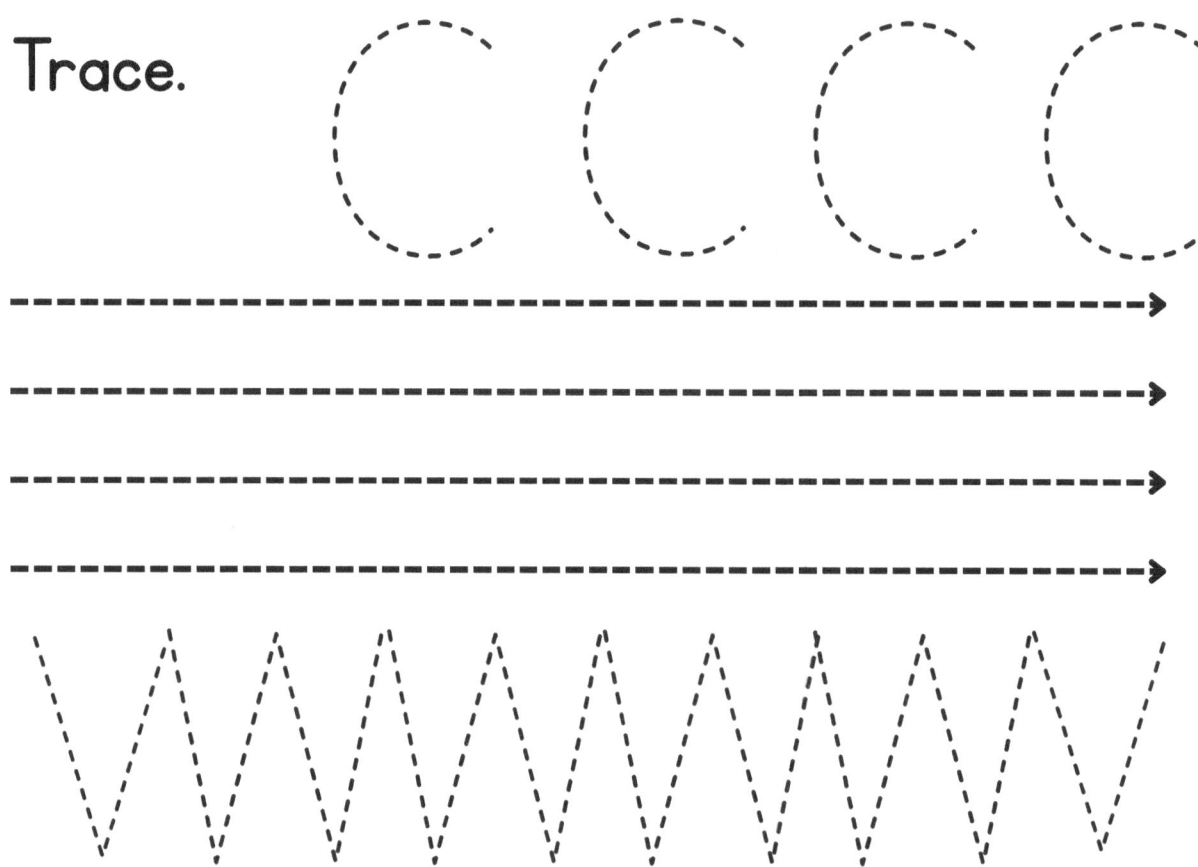

Find your way.

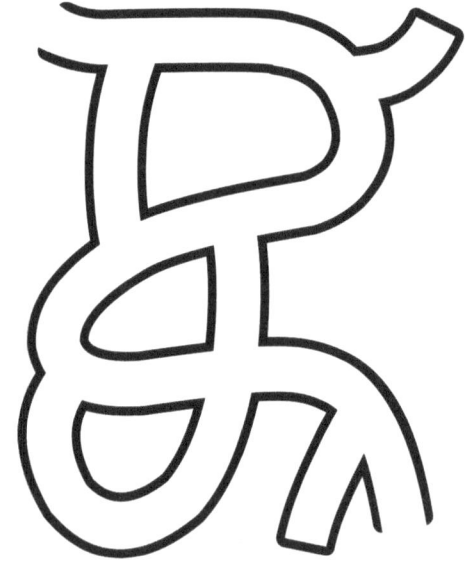

Ă ă

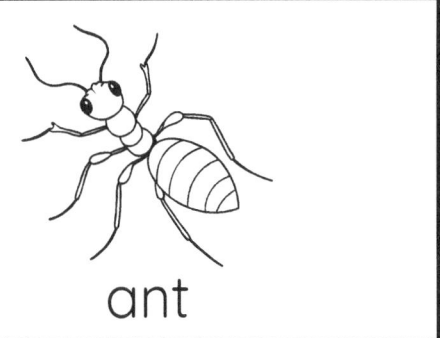
ant

Trace the letters.

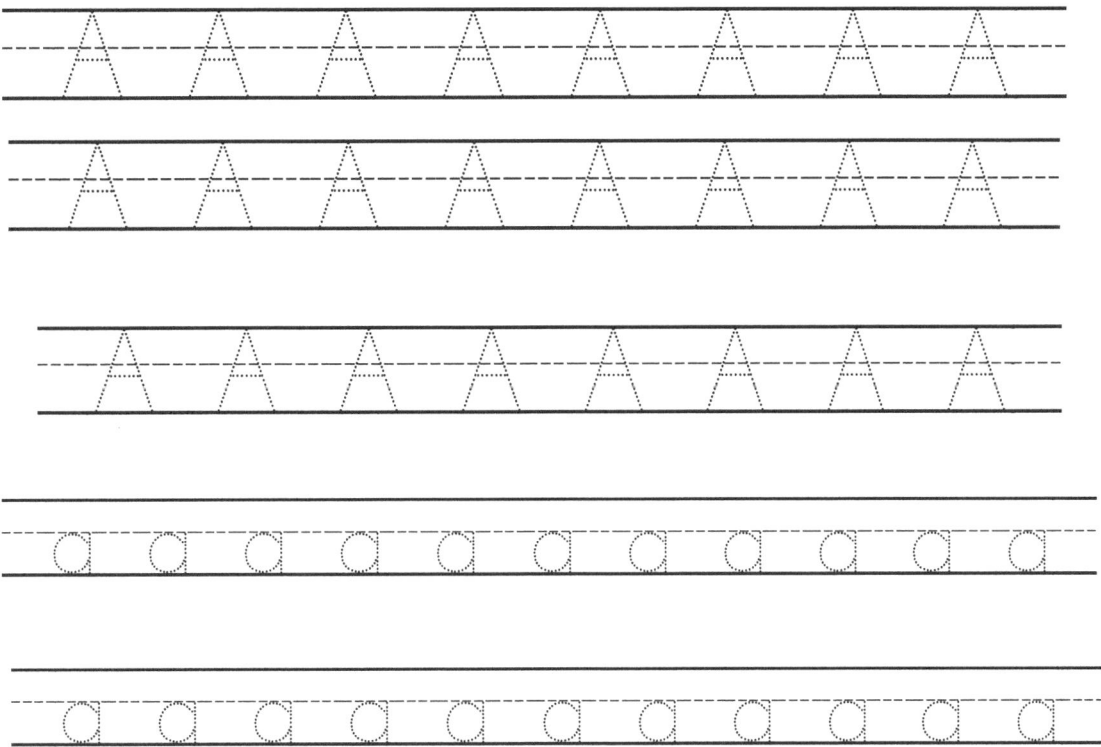

Circle A
A M x A f z C g A
b a s v I n F a c r
B k p h a j N e R

Circle a
A M x A f z C g A
b a s v I n F a c r
B k p h a j N e R

Color 5 pictures with the Ăă sound in red.

Trace.

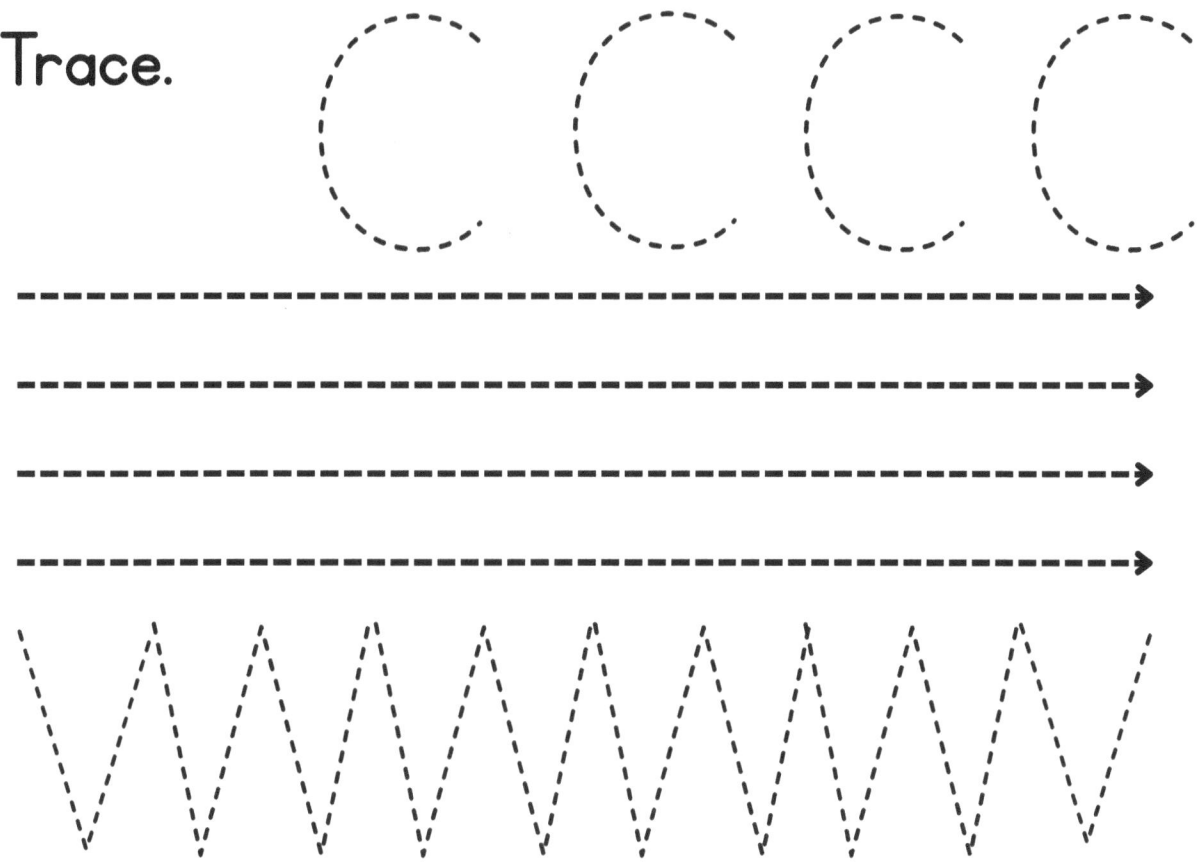

Find your way.

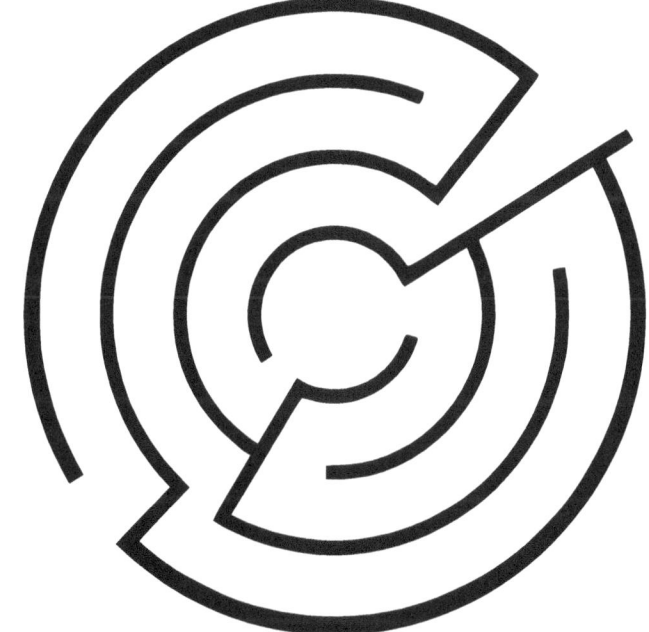

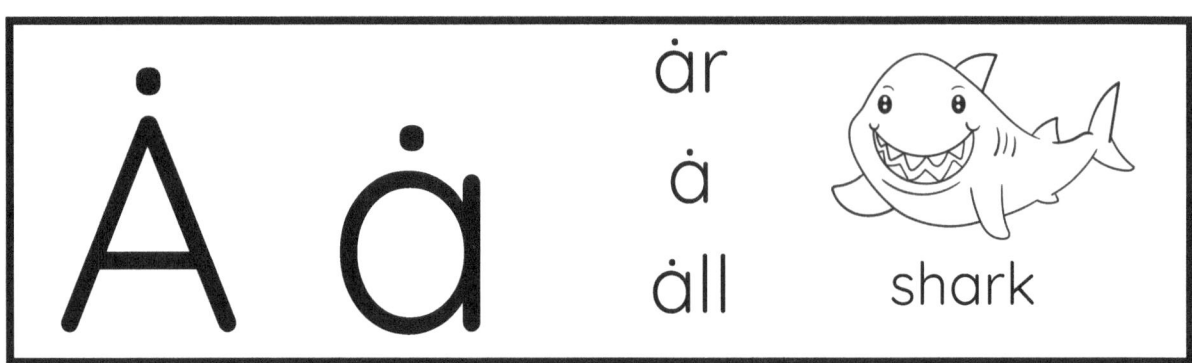

Ȧa ȧr ȧ ȧll shark

Trace the letters.

A A A A A A A
A A A A A A A
A A A A A A A

a a a a a a a a a a
a a a a a a a a a a

Circle a
B k p h a j N e R
b a s v l n F a c r
A M x A f z C g A

Circle A
B k p h a j N e R
b a s v l n F a c r
A M x A f z C g A

10

Color 4 pictures with the Àà sound in green.

Trace.

Match.

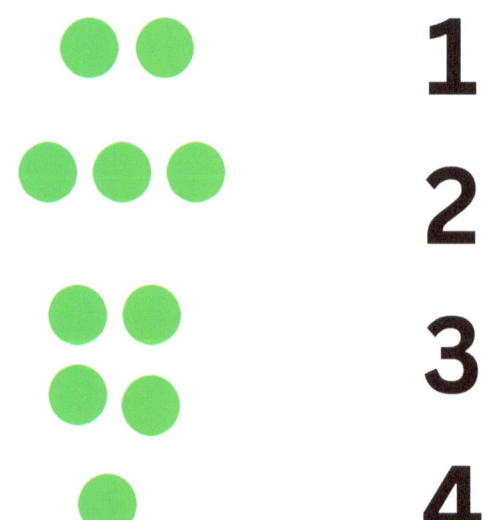

1

2

3

4

Trace the letters.

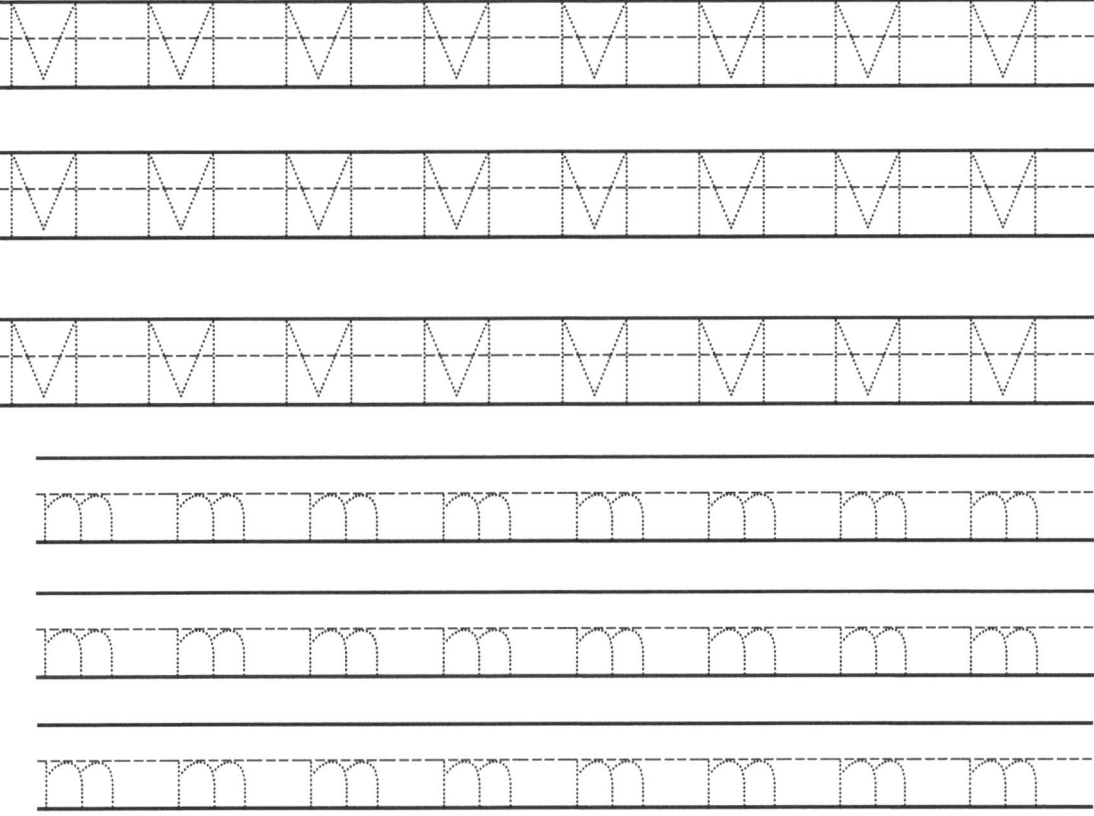

Circle M

A M x A f z C g A
b M s v l m F a c M
B k m h a j M e R

Circle m

A M x A f z M g A
b a m v l n m a c r
B k p M a j m e R

Color 5 pictures with the Mm sound in orange.

Sound and blend.

ăm   mā   màmà

Trace.

------------------→

------------------→

------------------→

Match.

1

2

3

4

5

S s

seal

Trace the letters.

Circle S

A S x A f z C g A
b M s v l m F a S M
S k m S a j M R s

Circle s

s M x A f z M g A
b a m v s n m f c r
B k s M a j m e S

16

Color 5 pictures with the Ss sound in yellow.

Sound and blend.

sā sām

Săm ăs Măss

Trace.

F f

frog

Trace the letters.

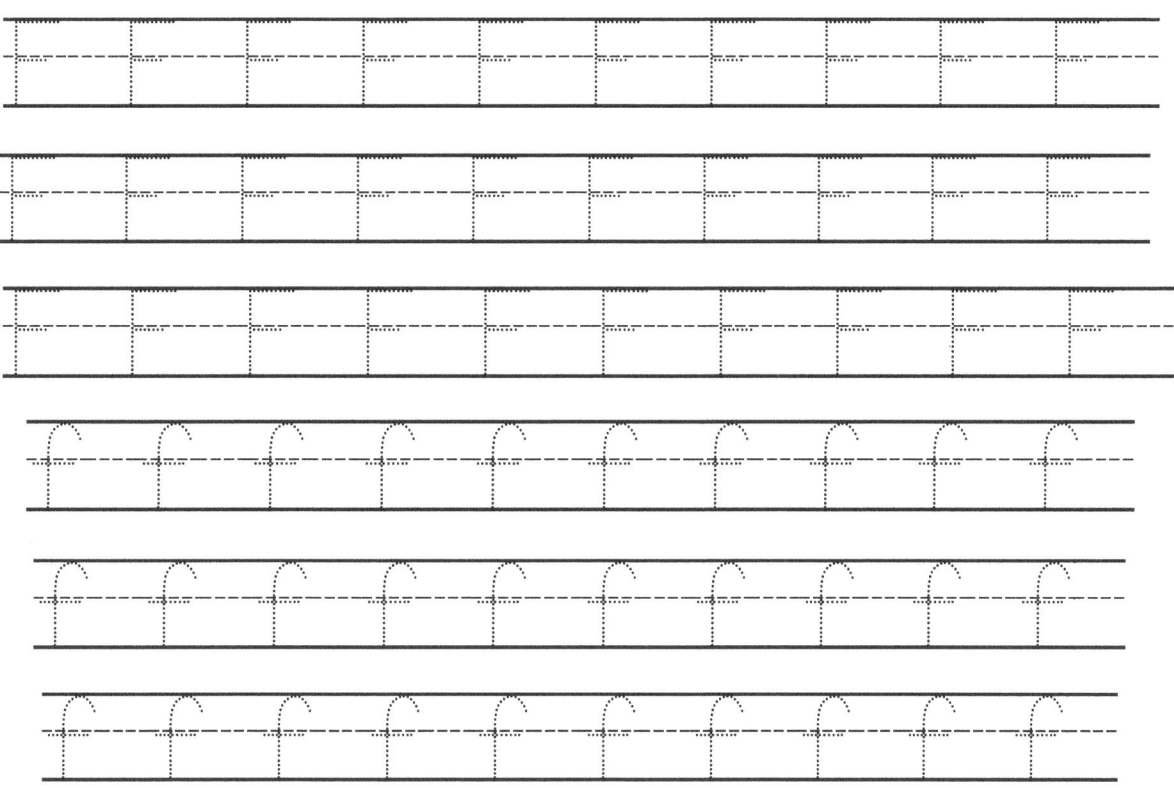

Circle F

F S x A f z C g A
f M s v F m F a S M
F k m S a j M F s

Circle f

s F x A f z M g A
b a m f s n m f c r
B f s M a j m e f

19

Color 4 pictures with the Ff sound in brown.

Sound and blend.

fām   sāf

Trace.

Match.

R r

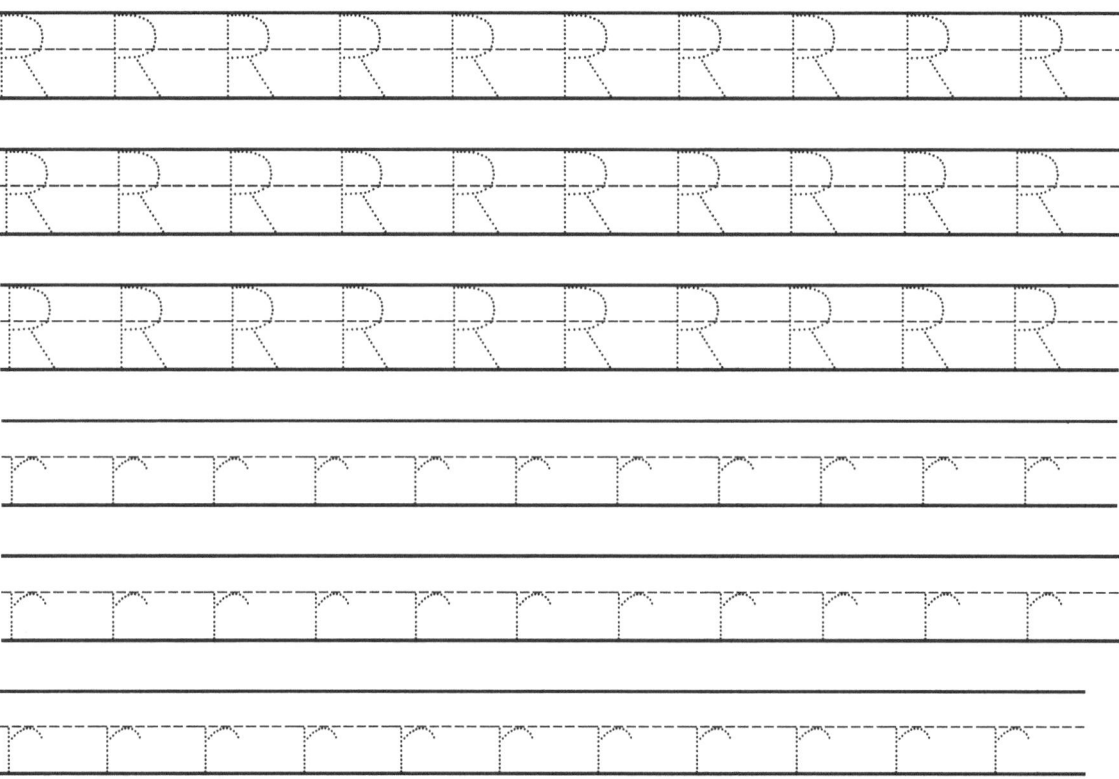

rabbit

Trace the letters.

Circle R

A R x A f z C g R
r M s l m R a S M
S R m S a j M R s

Circle r

r M x A f z M g r
b a m v r n m f c r
B k s F a j m r S

Color 5 pictures with the Rr sound in black.

Sound and blend.

rāy rări făre răm

ăr ăre Mărs

ărm făr fărm

Trace.

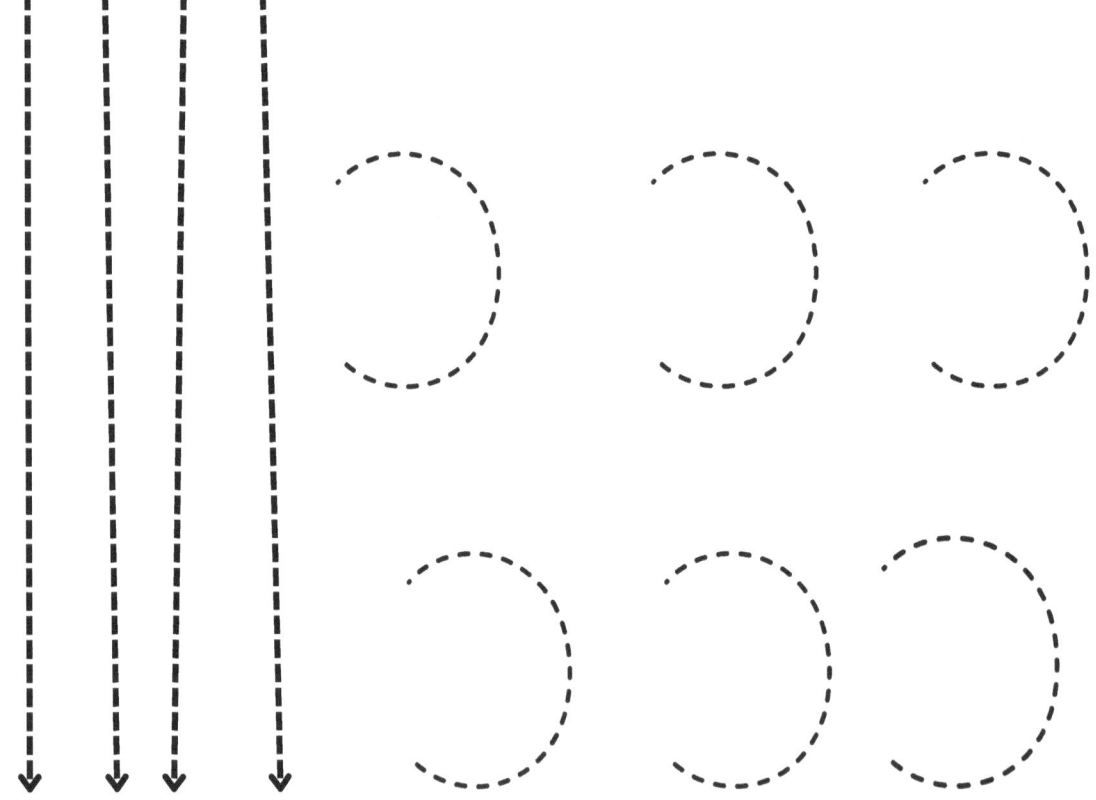

Trace the letters.

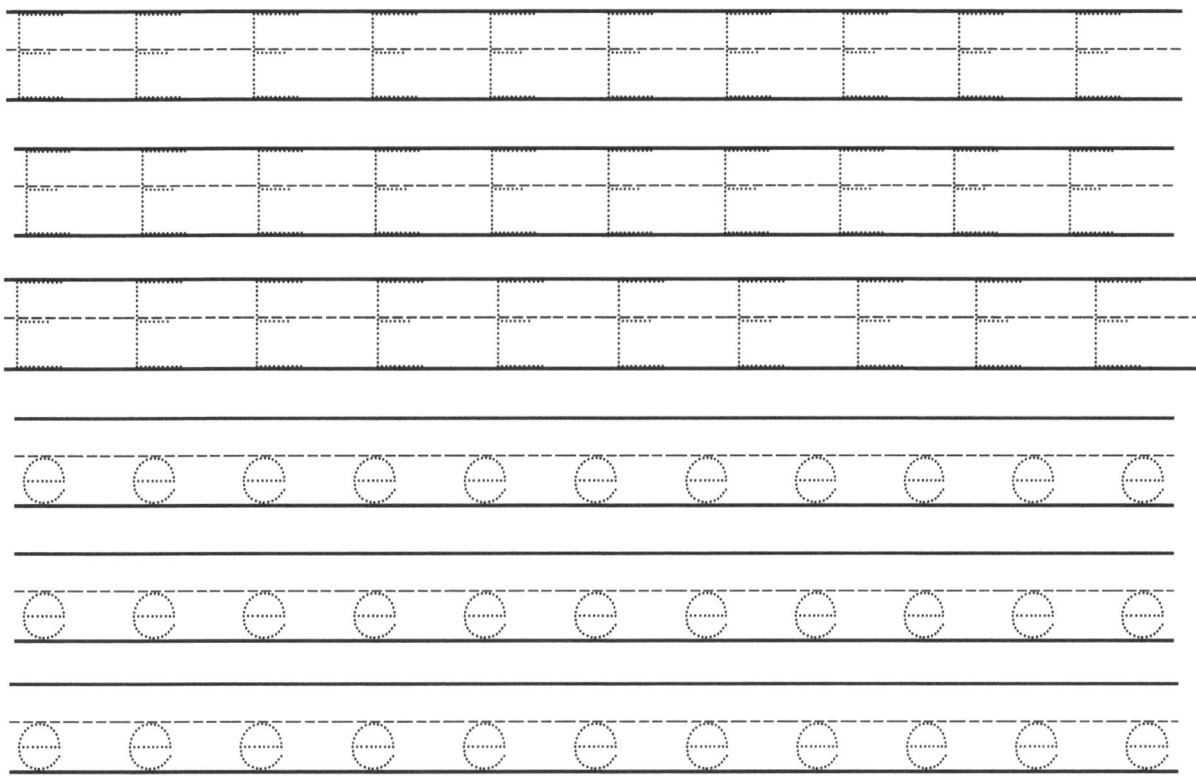

Circle E

E S x A f e C g A
b M s v E m F a E M
E k e S a j E R s

Circle e

s M x A e z M g A
b e m v s n E f c r
B k e M a j m e S

Color 5 pictures with the Ēē sound in red.

Sound and blend.

mē sēē fēē fēēt

sēa sē m ē r fē r

rēēf sēēm

Trace.

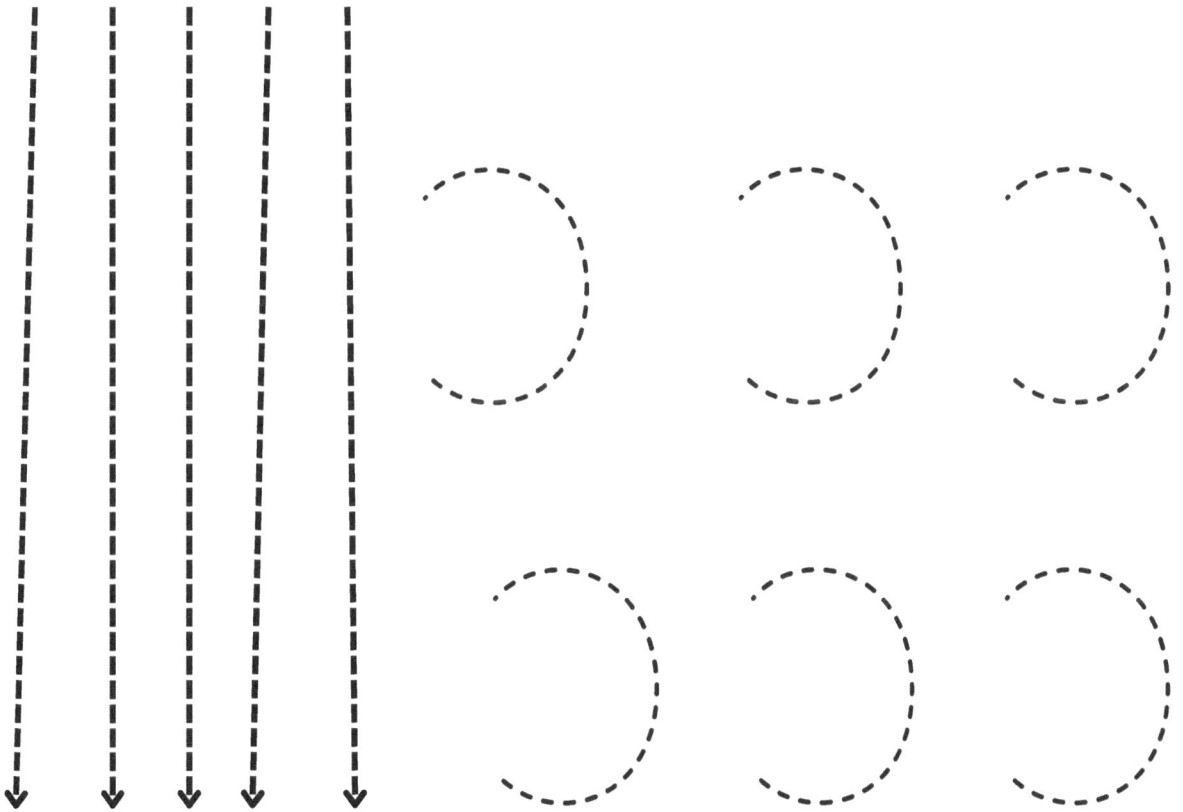

Trace the letters.

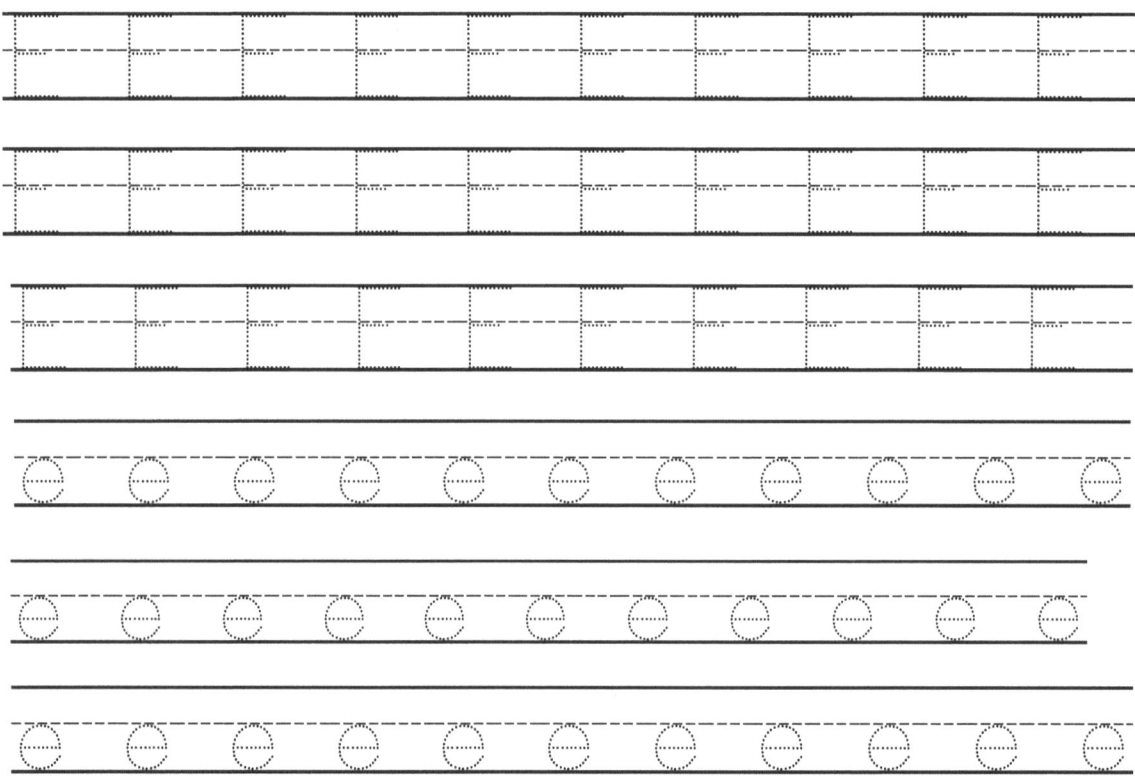

Circle E

E S x A f e C g A
b M s v E m F a E M
E k e S a j E R s

Circle e

s M x A e z M g A
b e m v s n E f c r
B k e M a j m e S

Color 4 pictures with the Ĕĕ sound in purple.

Sound and blend.

ĕrȧ

Trace.

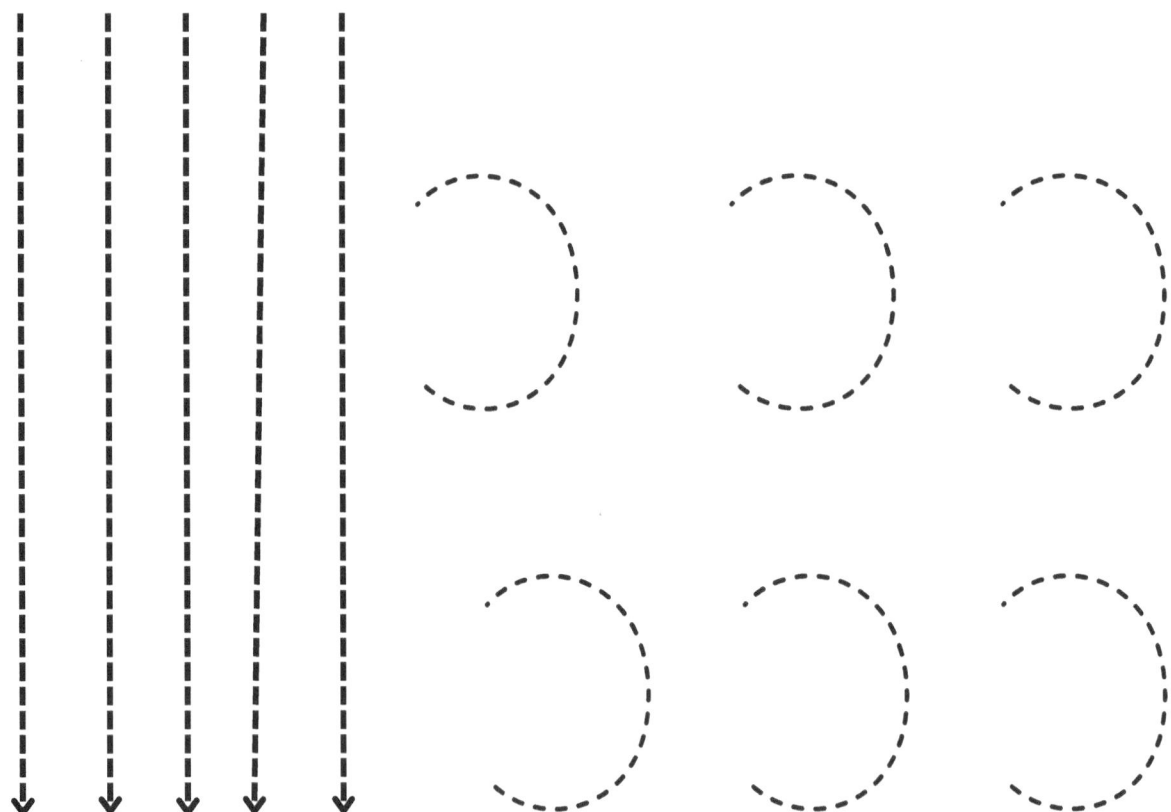

B b

bear

Trace the letters.

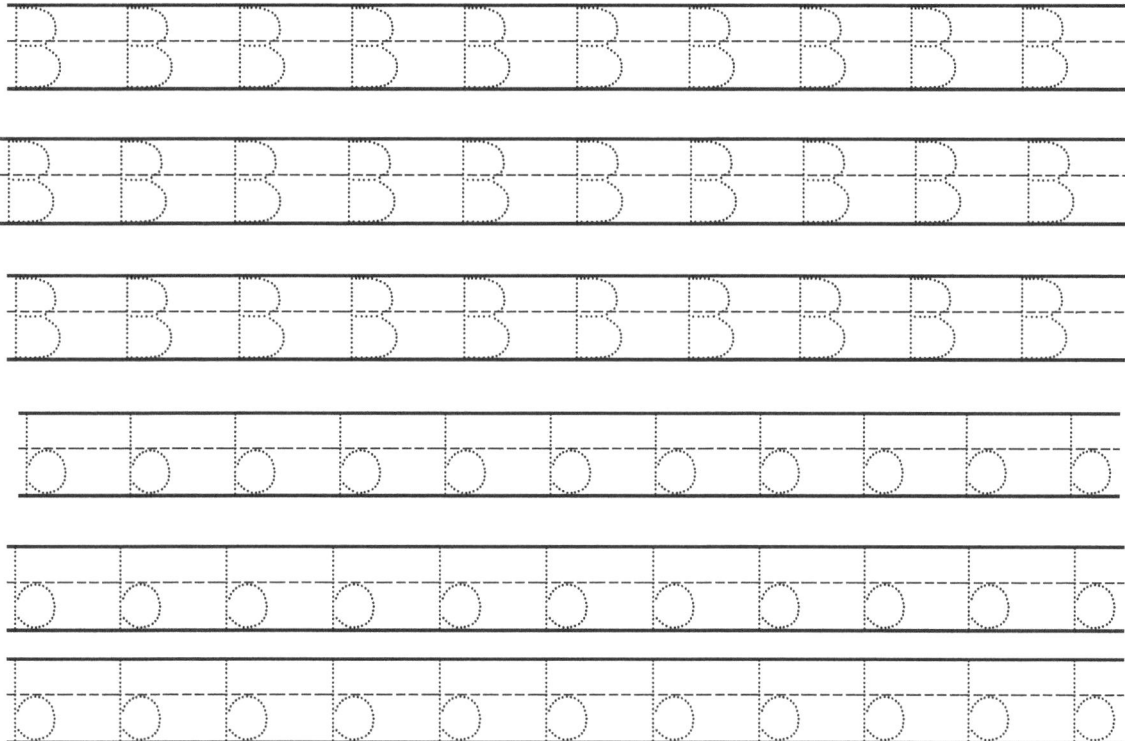

Circle B

A B x A f z C g A
b M s v B m F a B M
S k B S a j M R b

Circle b

s M x A f z b g A
b a m v s b m f c r
B k s M a j b e S

Color 4 pictures with the Bb sound in yellow.

Sound and blend.

bāy bāse bāss

Ābē bē bēē bēēf

bȧr bȧbȧ bēam

Trace.

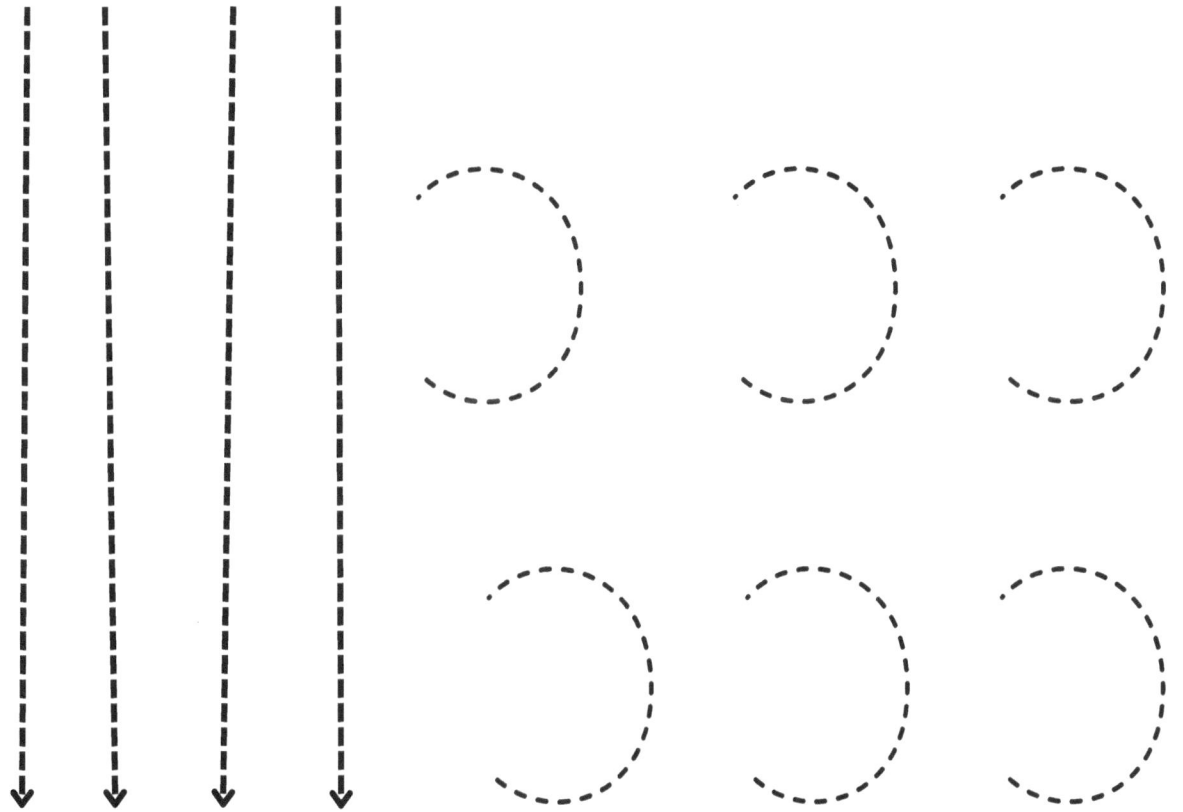

N n
nightingale

Trace the letters.

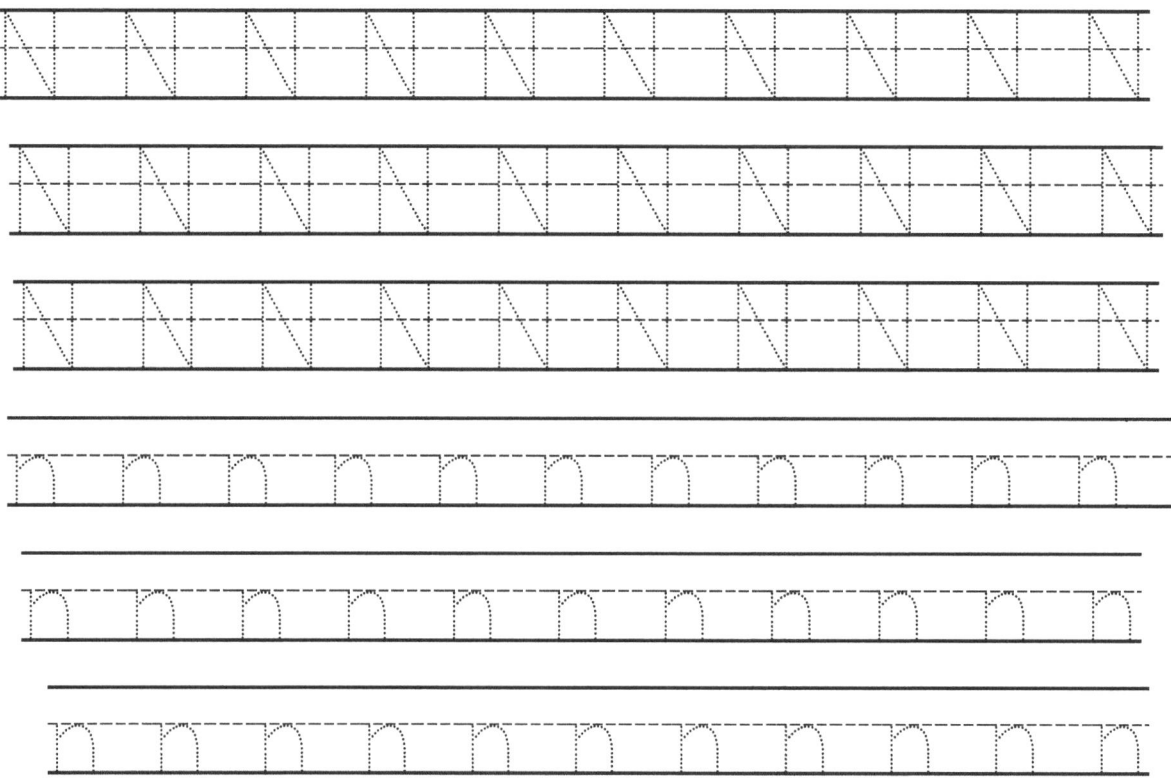

Circle N

N B x A f z C g A
b N s v B m F a N M
S k B N a j M R b

Circle n

s M x n f z b g A
b a m v s b n f c n
B k n M a j b e S

Color 4 pictures with the Nn sound in blue.

Sound and blend.

nām fām sām

mē n bēēn sēēn

ăn făn răn măn měn

Read and copy.

name   fame   same

mean   been   seen

an   fan   ran

man   men

Rule: The silent 'e' makes a say its name. e.g
căp cāp .

Double ee says ē.

Ḡ ḡ

giraffe

Trace the letters.

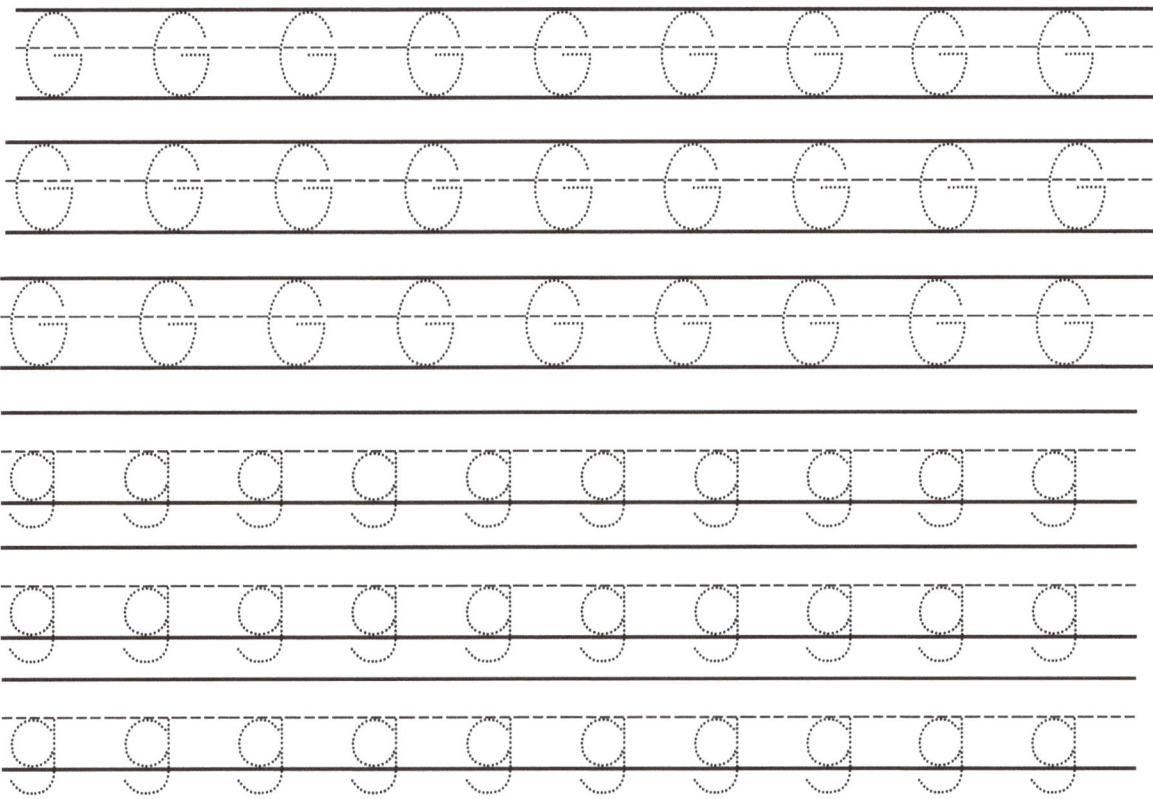

Circle Gg

A G x A f z C g A
b G s v B m F a B g
G k B S a g M R b

Rule: G says ḡ before e, i, y

Color 4 pictures with the Ḡḡ sound in yellow.

Sound and blend.

āḡ   sāḡ   rāḡ   ḡĕm

Read, trace and copy.

age   sage

rage   gem

Rule: G says ḡ before e, i, y.

goat

Trace the letters.

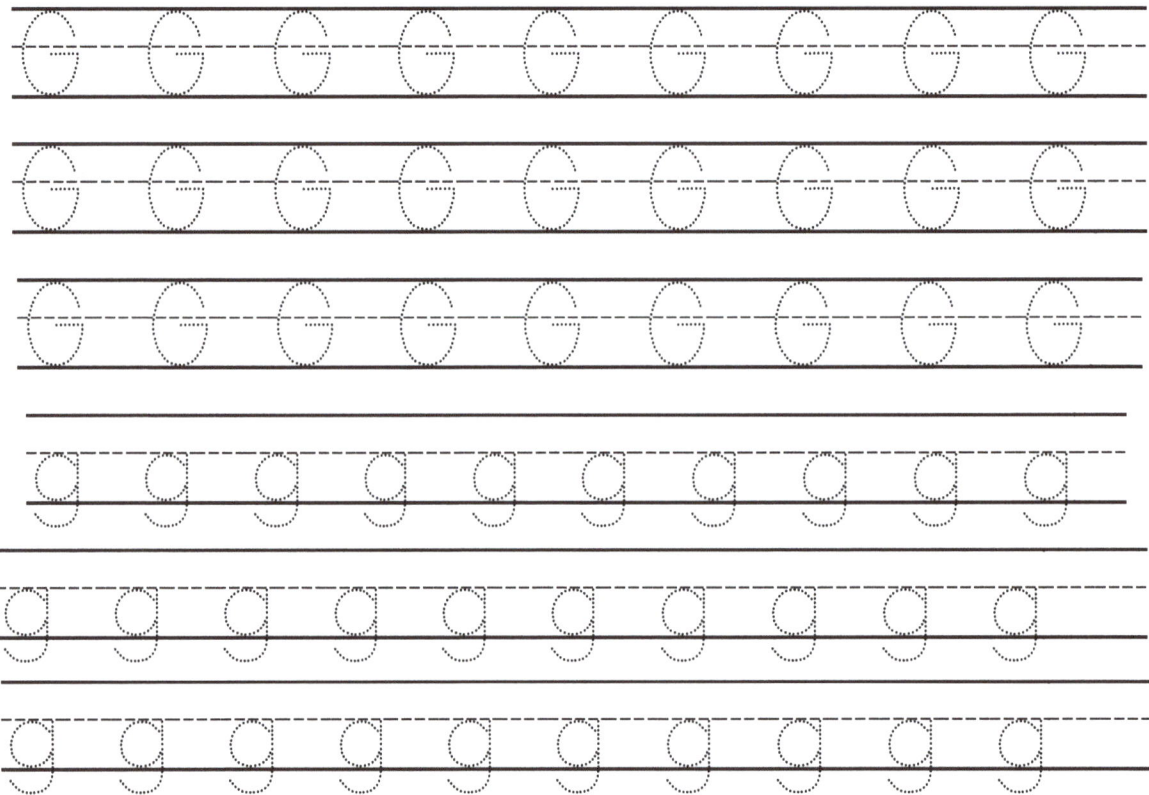

Circle Gg

A G x A f z C g A
b G s v B m F a B g
G k B S a g M R b

Rule: G says ğ before a, o, u or a consonant

Color 4 pictures with the Ğğ sound in orange.

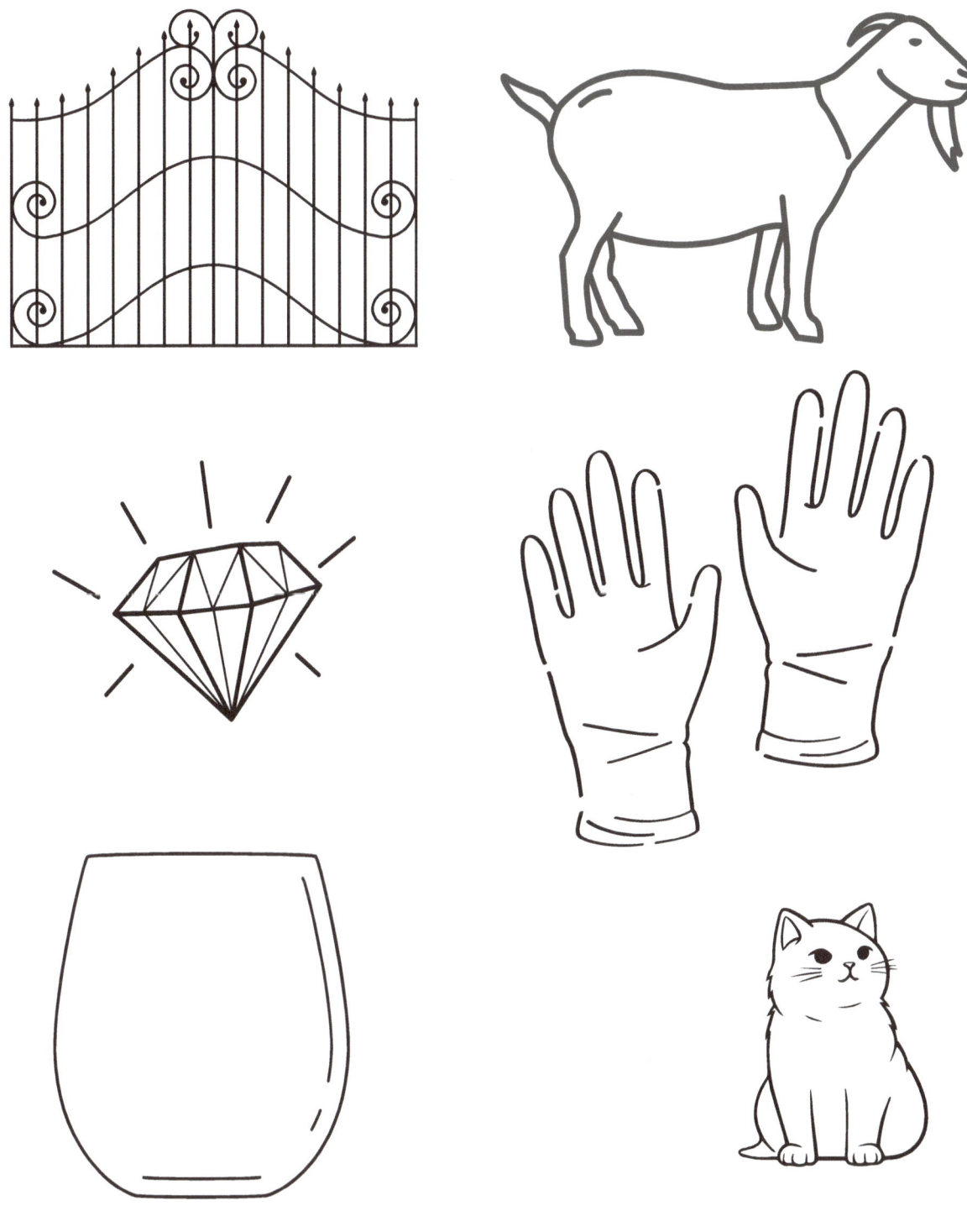

Sound and blend.

ğām   ğärb   ğăs

ĕğğ   bĕğ   băğ

Read, trace and copy.

game   garb

gas   egg

beg   bag

Rule: G says ğ before a, o, u.

T t

tiger

Trace the letters.

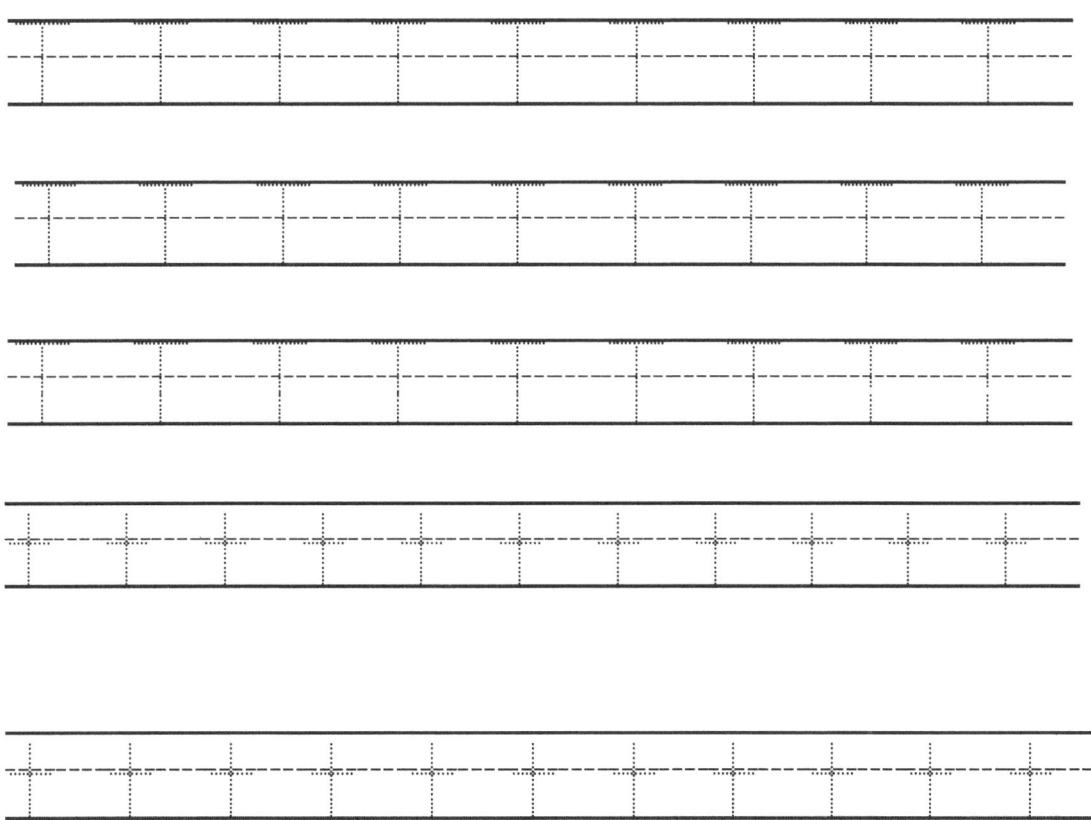

Circle T

A T x A f z C g A
b M s v B T F a B M
S k B T a j M R t

Circle t

s M x t f z b g A
b a m v s b t f c r
B k t M a j b e T

Color 4 pictures with the Tt sound in red.

Sound and blend.

ăt măt băt răt săt făt
sĕt nĕt mĕt ğĕt tĕn
āt fāt ğāt rāt tām

Read, trace and copy.

at   mat   bat   rat

sat   fat   set   net

met   get   ten   ate

fate   gate   rate   tame

Sound and blend.

tăn tăb tăg răt tàr

ē t mē t sēat běst něst rěst

tē m   tē r tē s

mēēt fēēt bēēt

Read, trace and copy.

tan   tab   tag   rat

tar   eat   meat   seat

best   nest   rest   team

tear   tear   tease

meet   feet   beet

P p

parrot

Trace the letters.

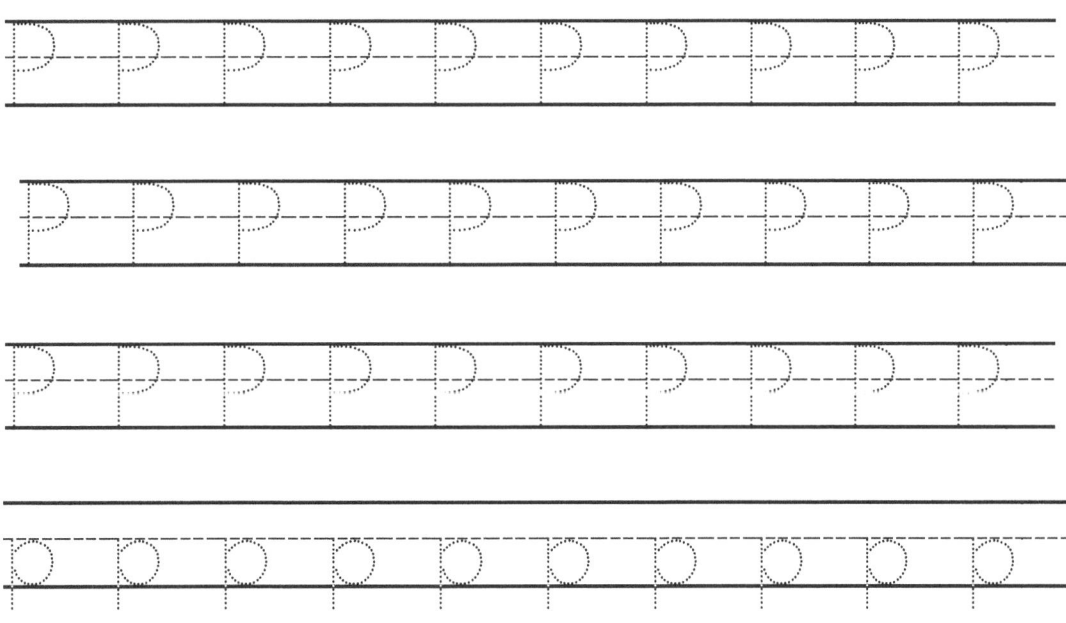

Circle P

P T x A f z C g P
b M s v B P F a B M
S k P T a j M R p

Circle p

s p x P f z b g A
p a m v p b t f c r
B k t M p j b e T

Color 5 pictures with the Pp sound in pink.

Sound and blend.

sēēp bēēp pēēp rē p

āp tāp pā pāḡ pān pāst

Read, trace and copy.

seep			beep

peep			reap

ape		tape		pay

page		pane		paste

Trace the letters.

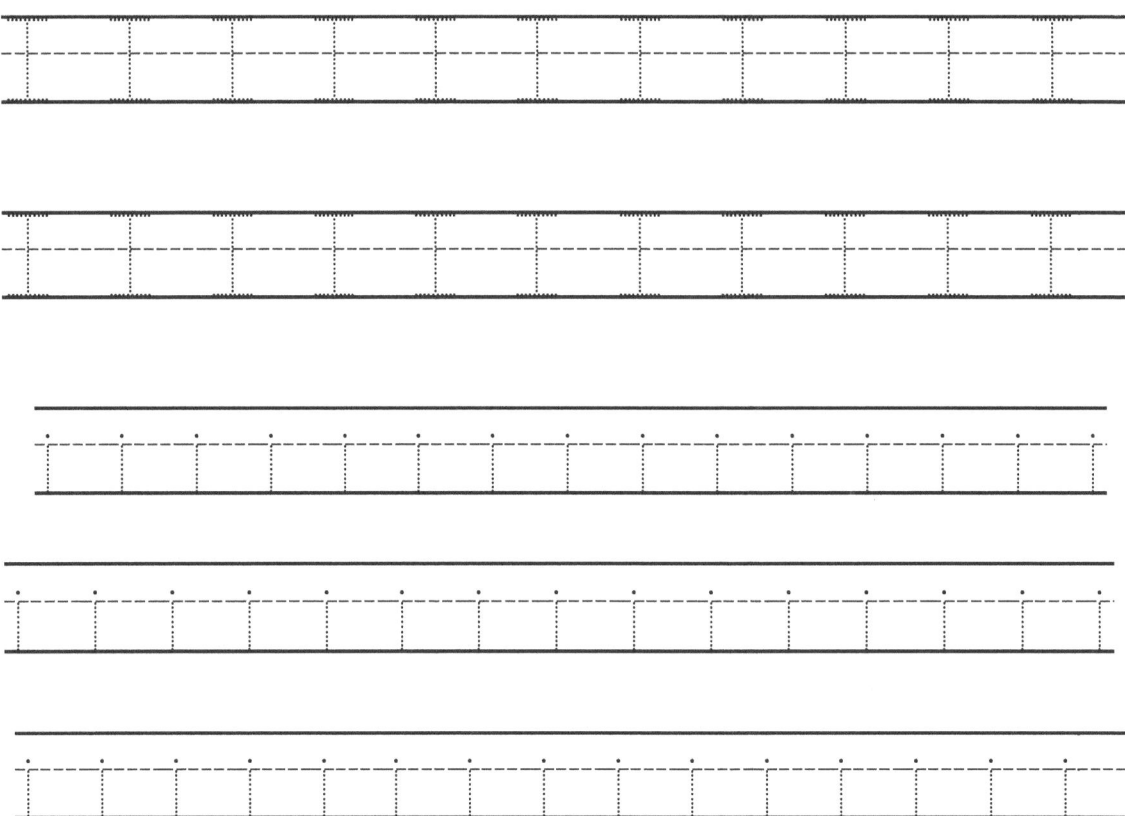

Circle I

A T x A f z C g I
I M i v B T I a B M
i k B T a I M R t

Circle i

s i x t f z b g I
b a i v s b i f c r
B k t M a i b e T

Color 4 pictures with the Īī sound in purple.

51

Sound and blend.

pī   tī   fīn   mīn   nīn   pīn

bīt   mīt   sīt   tīm   prīm   grīm

Read, trace and copy.

pie   tie   fine

mine   nine   pine

bite   mite   site

time   prime   grime

Sound and blend.

fīr mīr tīr

nī t mī t sī t tī t trī t fī t

Read, trace and copy.

fire   mire   tire

night   might

sight   tight

right   fight

iguana

Trace the letters.

Circle I

A T x A f z C g I
I M i v B T I a B M
i k B T a I M R t

Circle i

s i x t f z b g I
b a i v s b i f c r
B k t M a i b e T

Color 4 pictures with the Ĭĭ sound in yellow.

55

Sound and blend.

fĭt sĭt pĭt bĭt fĭst mĭst

nĭp sĭp rĭp pĭp tĭp

Read, trace and copy.

fit   sit   pit

fist   mist

nip   sip   rip

pip   tip

Sound and blend.

pĭg bĭg fĭg rĭg bĭb rĭb
stĭff pĭn sĭn fĭn tĭn bĭn

Read, trace and copy.

pig　　　　　big　　　　　fig

rig　　　　　bib　　　　　rib

stiff　　　　　pin　　　　　sin

fin　　　　　tin　　　　　bin

D d

duck

Trace the letters.

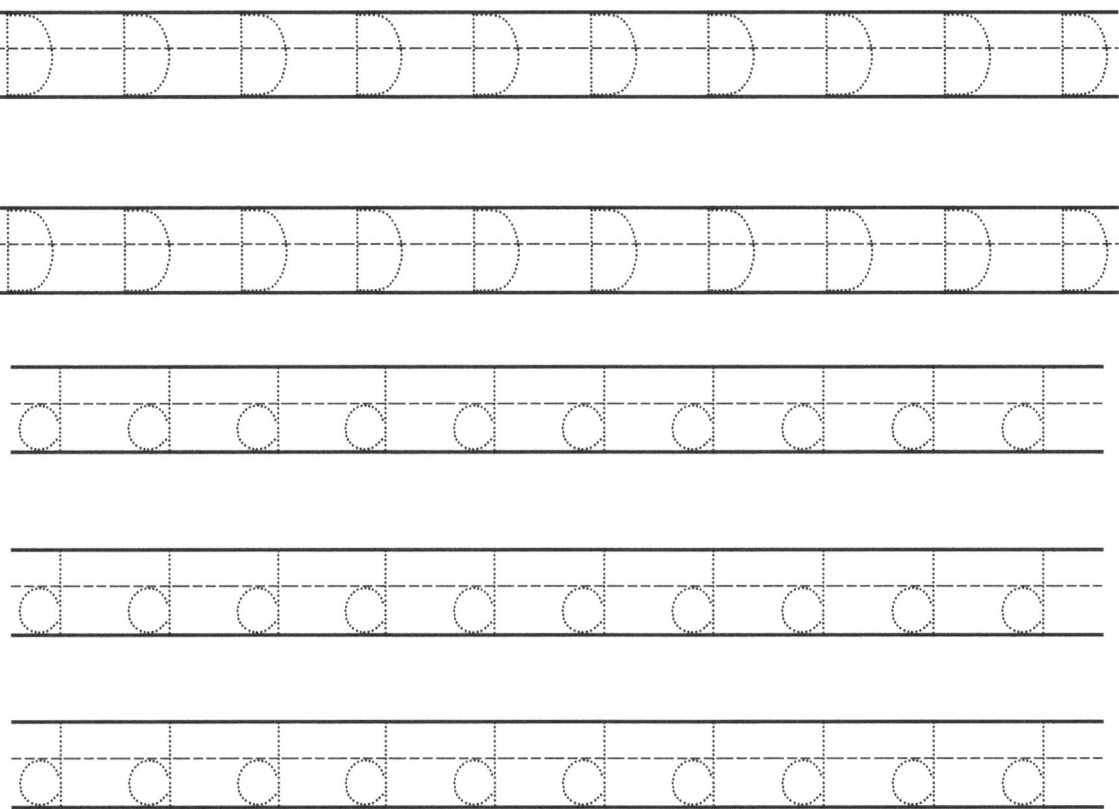

Circle D

D T x A f d C g A
b D s v D T F a B M
S k B T a j M R D

Circle d

d M x t f z b g A
b d D v s b d f c r
B d t M a j b e d

Color 4 pictures with the Dd sound in brown.

Sound and blend.

dāy āid rāid pāid māid
māde dāte fāde trāde

Read, trace and copy.

day　　　　　　　aid　　　　　　　raid

paid　　　　　　　　　　　　　　　maid

made　　　　　　　　　　　　　　date

fade　　　　　　　　　　　　　　trade

Sound and blend.

măd dăd băd făd săd păd
sēēd dēēd nēēd rēēd fēēd
dēēp

Read, trace and copy.

mad　　　　　dad　　　　　bad

fad　　　　　sad　　　　　pad

seed　　　　deed　　　　need

reed　　　　feed　　　　deep

Sound and blend.

běd fěd rěd měnd sěnd běnd

rĭd dĭd dĭp dĭm dīme rīde sīde
tīde

Read, trace and copy.

bed   fed   red

mend   send   bend

rid   did   dip

dim   dime   ride

side   tide

Trace the letters.

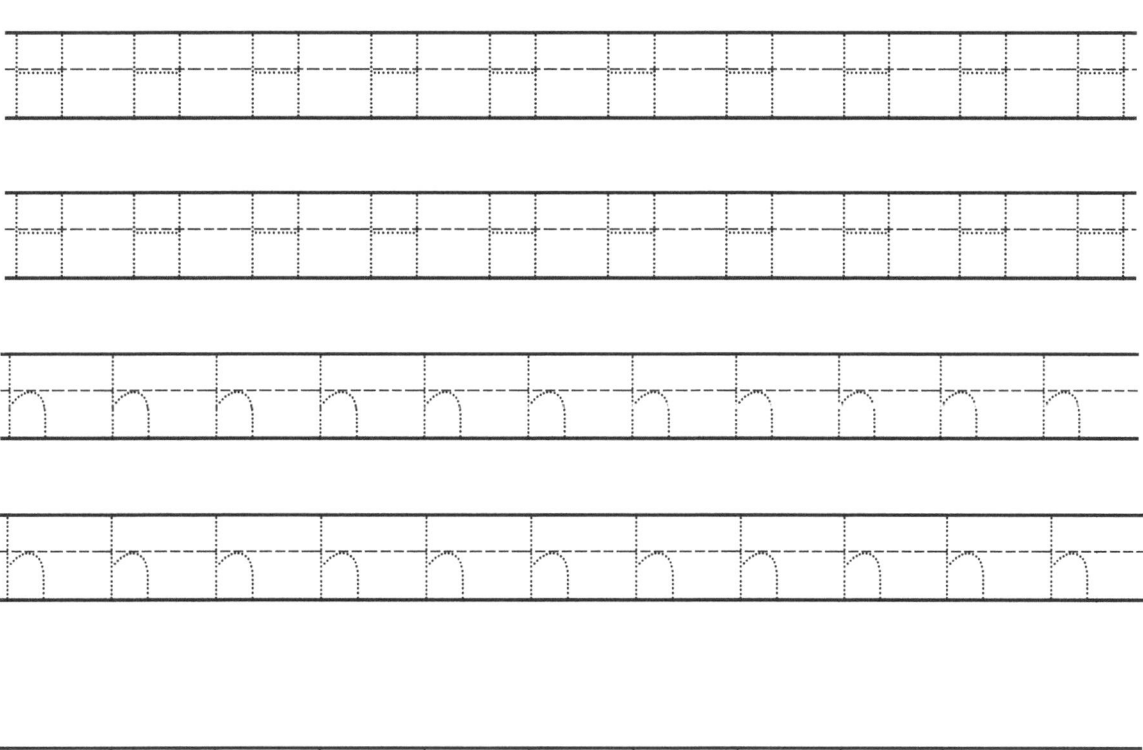

Circle H

D H x A f d C g A
b h s v H T F a B H
S k H T a j M H D

Circle h

d h x t f z b h A
b d D v s h n f c r
H d t h a j b e H

Color 4 pictures with the Hh sound in purple.

Sound and blend.

hē hear heat heart hård

hålt hĕad hĕn hĕdge

Read, trace and copy.

he   hear   heat

heart   hard

halt   head

hen   hedge

Sound and blend.

hāy hāte hăt hăs hăd hănd
hăir hī hīde hĭll hĭm

Read, trace and copy.

hay　　　hate　　　hat

has　　　had　　　hand

hair　　　hi　　　hide

hill　　　him

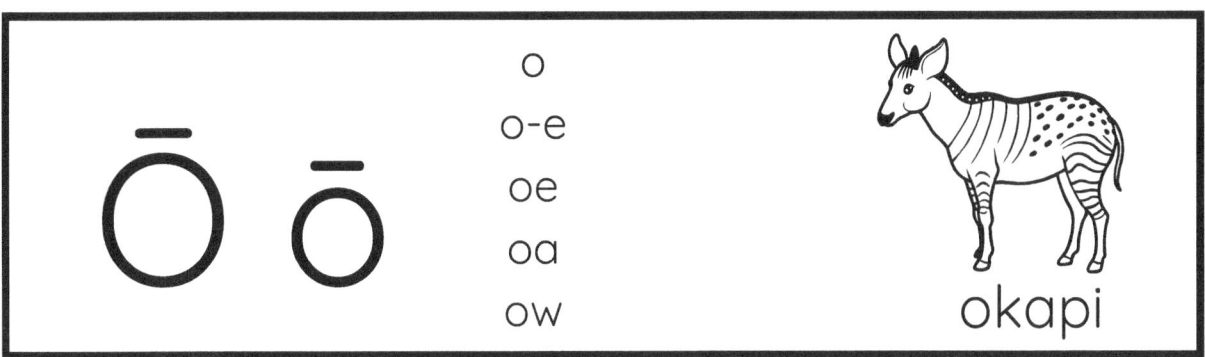

Trace the letters.

Circle O

D H o A f d O g A
b h s v O T F a B H
O k H o a j M O D

Circle o

O h x o f z b o A
o d D v o h n f D r
O d t h o j b e H

Color 4 pictures with the Ōō sound in yellow.

Sound and blend.

nō sō ğō hōe tōe dōe fōe

hōme dōme pōle mōle rōle

Read, trace and copy.

no　　　　so　　　　go

hoe　　　　toe　　　　doe

foe　　　　home　　　　dome

pole　　　　mole　　　　role

Sound and blend.

sōle rōpe hōpe lōne bōne

nōse hōse rōse pōst mōst

Read, trace and copy.

sole   rope   hope

lone   bone   nose

hose   rose

post   most

Sound and blend.

hōst bōat rōad tōad nōte
mōde sōap fōam rōam sōak

Read, trace and copy.

host   boat   road

toad   note   mode

mode   foam   soap

roam   soak

Trace the letters.

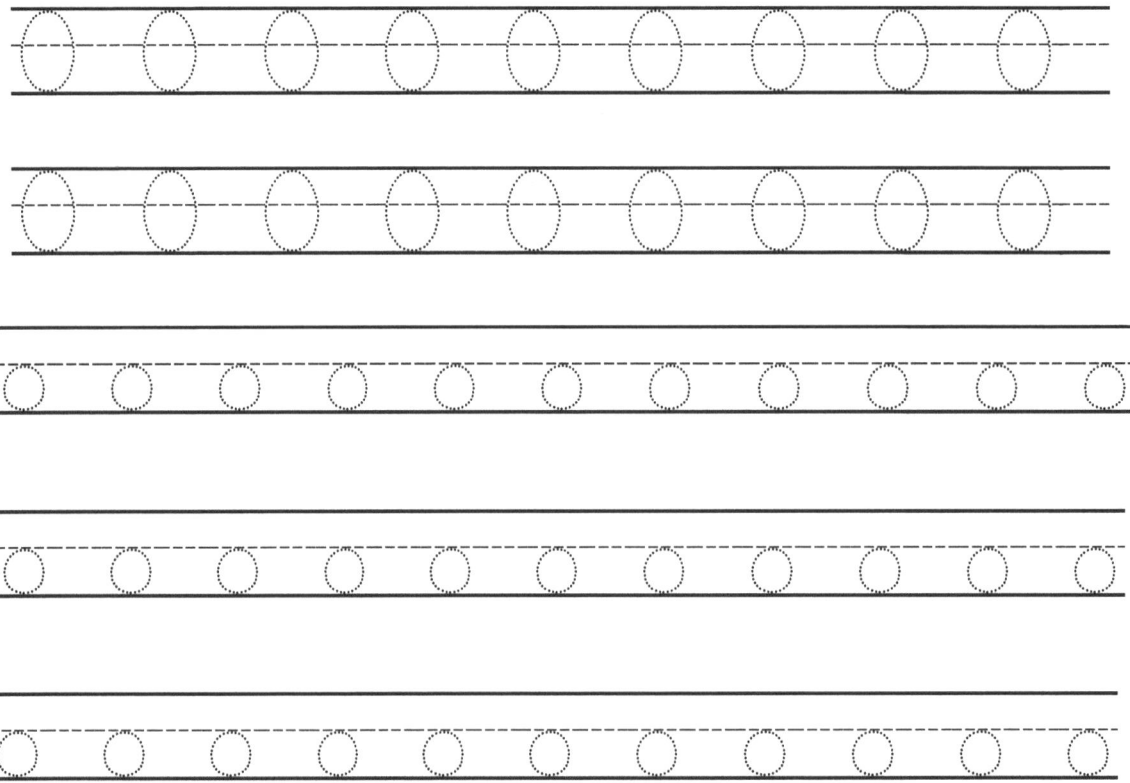

Circle O

D H o A f d O g A
b h s v O T F a B H
O k H o a j M O D

Circle o

O h x o f z b o A
o d D v o h n f D r
O d t h o j b e H

Color 4 pictures with the Ŏŏ sound in brown.

Sound and blend.

ğŏt hŏt nŏt dŏt tŏt pŏt

rŏt dŏğ fŏğ smŏğ mŏb sŏb

Read, trace and copy.

got　　　　　hot　　　　　not

dot　　　　　tot　　　　　pot

rot　　　　　dog　　　　　fog

smog　　　　mob　　　　　sob

Sound and blend.

rŏb tŏp hŏp mŏp pŏp sŏd

nŏd pŏd rŏd Gŏd pŏnd bŏnd

Read, trace and copy.

rob　　　　top　　　　hop

mop　　　　pop　　　　sod

nod　　　　pod　　　　rod

God　　　　pond　　　　bond

Sound and blend.

bŏss mŏss tŏss stŏp

frŏg trŏt trŏd drŏp

Read, trace and copy.

boss　　　　　　　　　　　　　　　moss

toss　　　　　　　　　　　　　　　stop

frog　　　　　　　　　　　　　　　trot

trod　　　　　　　　　　　　　　　drop

Trace the letters.

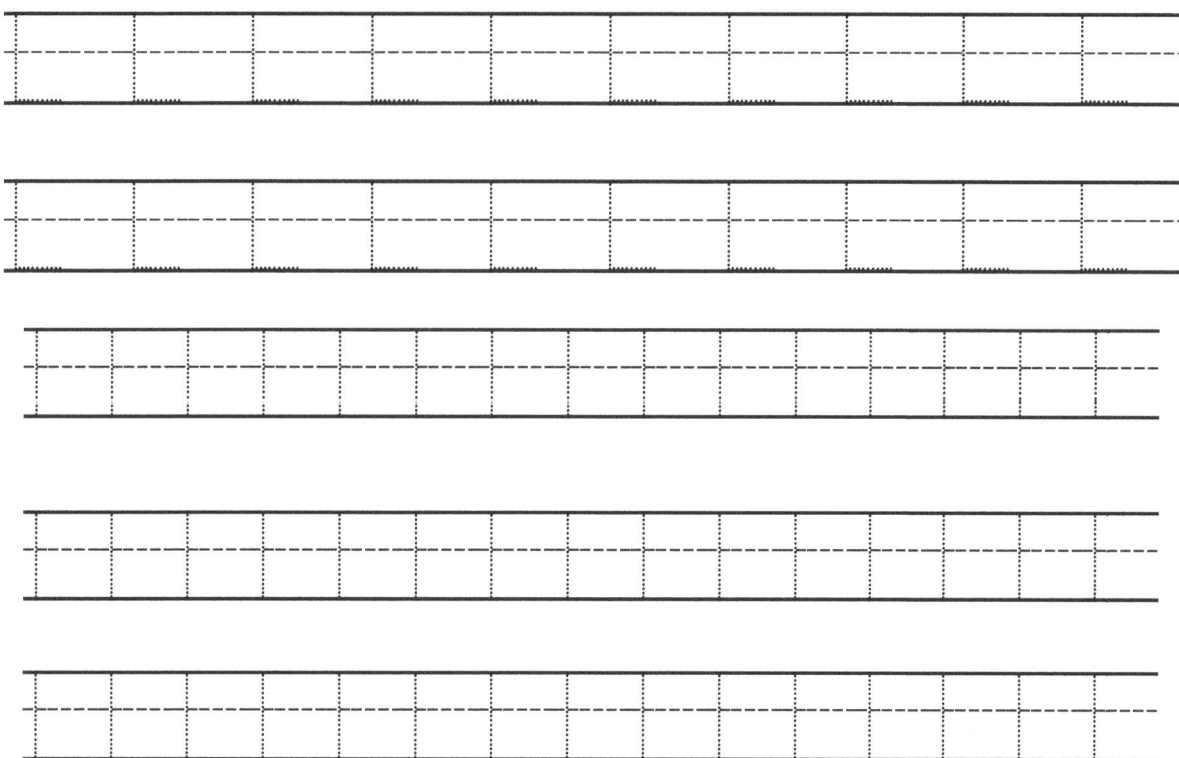

Circle L

D H o L f d O g A
L h s v O T L a B H
I k L o a j M O L

Circle l

O h x l f z l o A
o d D v L h n f l r
O l t h o j l e H

Color 4 pictures with the Ll sound in blue.

Sound and blend.

tāle māle pāle bāle sāle ğāle
bȧll fȧll hȧll tȧll mȧll fēēl

Read, trace and copy.

tate   mate   pate

bate   sate   gate

ball   fall   hall

tall   mall   feel

Sound and blend.

pēēl   rēēl   fĕll   sĕll   bĕll   tĕll
līne   līke   hōle   pōle   sōle   mōle

Read, trace and copy.

peel   reel   fell

sell   bell   tell

line   like   hole

pole   sole   mole

Sound and blend.

hĭll bĭll fĭll mĭll dĭll sĭll

ğōal lōaf lŏt lŏft lŏğ lŏss

Read, trace and copy.

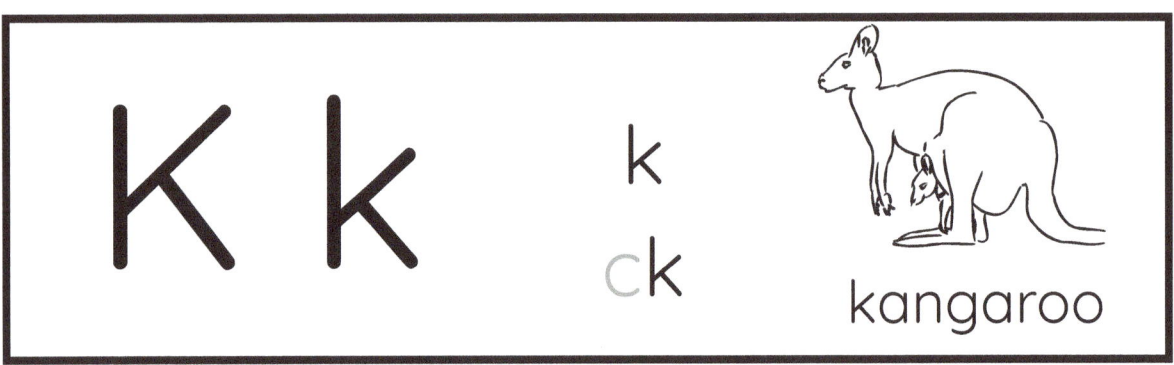

Trace the letters.

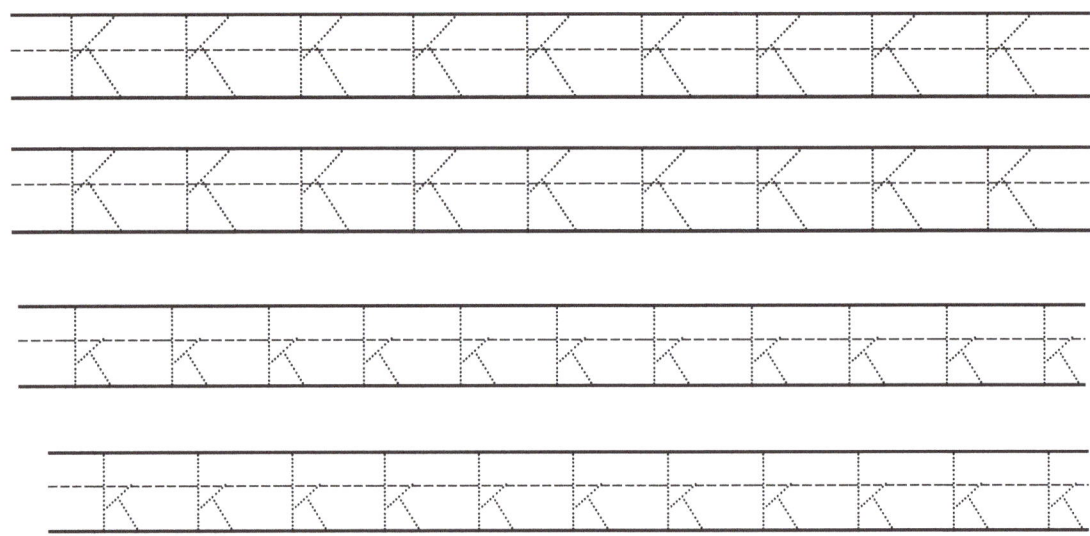

Short vowel? Use "ck" e.g rŏck
Long vowel or consonant before? Use "k"
e.g book & wēēk. Note: There are exception.

Draw a line to match the picture with the first sound

Color 5 pictures with the Kk sound in green.

Sound and blend.

bāke māke tāke rāke fāke
lāke sāke kĭt

bēak pēak

Read, trace and copy.

bake   make   take

rake   fake   lake

sake   kit

beak   peak

Sound and blend.

līke hīke pīke hīke bīke spīke

kīnd kīte īnk sīnk pīnk līnk

Read, trace and copy.

līke   hīke   pīke

hīke   bīke   spīke

kīnd   kīte   īnk

sīnk   pīnk   līnk

Sound and blend.

mĭnk rĭnk drĭnk sĭlk mĭlk kĭd

kĭck tĭck sĭck lĭck pĭck rŏck

Read, trace and copy.

mink　　　　　rink　　　　　drink

silk　　　　　milk　　　　　kid

kick　　　　　tick　　　　　sick

tick　　　　　pick　　　　　rock

Sight words

the   to   is

Read.

Nĕd thĕ Măn

Nĕd ĭs ā măn.

Hē hăd ā dŏg.

Thĕ dŏg hăd ā tăg.

Hē răn to thĕ măt.

Nĕd lĕt thĕ dŏg sĭt.

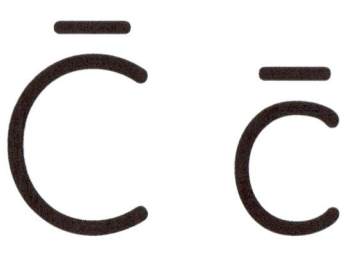

camel

Trace the letters.

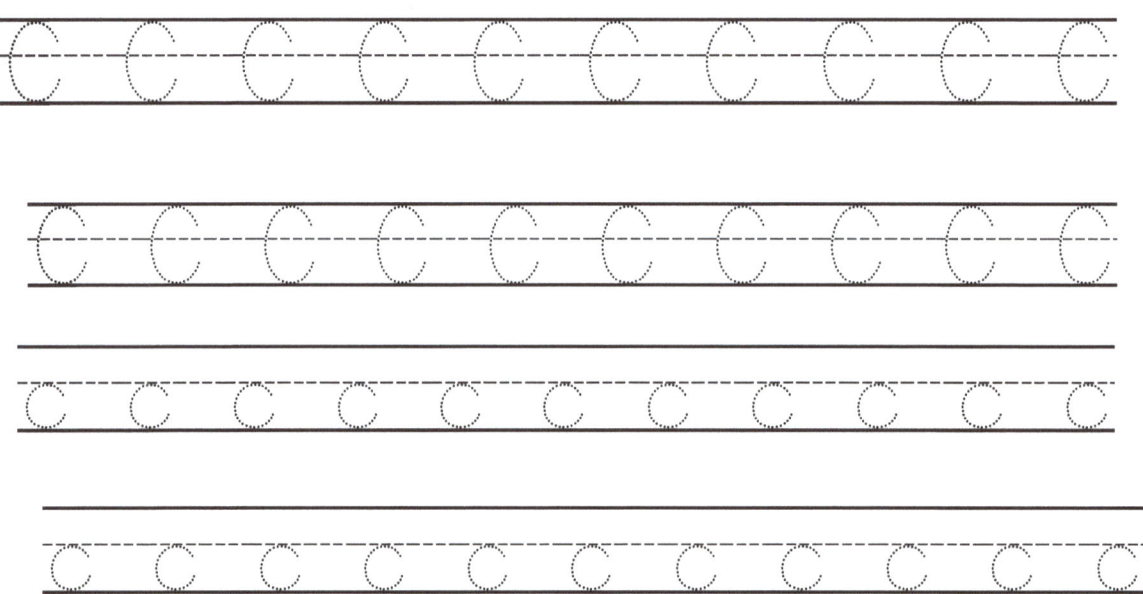

C makes the /k/ sound when it comes before:

a, o, u, or other consonants

Draw a line to match the picture with the first sound

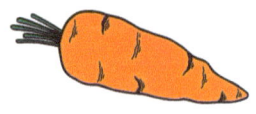   c      p

   b      c

Color 4 pictures with the C̄c̄ sound in yellow.

Sound and blend.

cāke cāme cāse cāpe

căn căp căt căr

Read, trace and copy.

cake   came

case   cape

can   cap

cat   car

Sound and blend.

cārd cŏd cŏb cŏt

cōmb cōne cŏrn cāge

Read, trace and copy.

card   cod

cob   cot

comb   cone

corn   cage

Trace the letters.

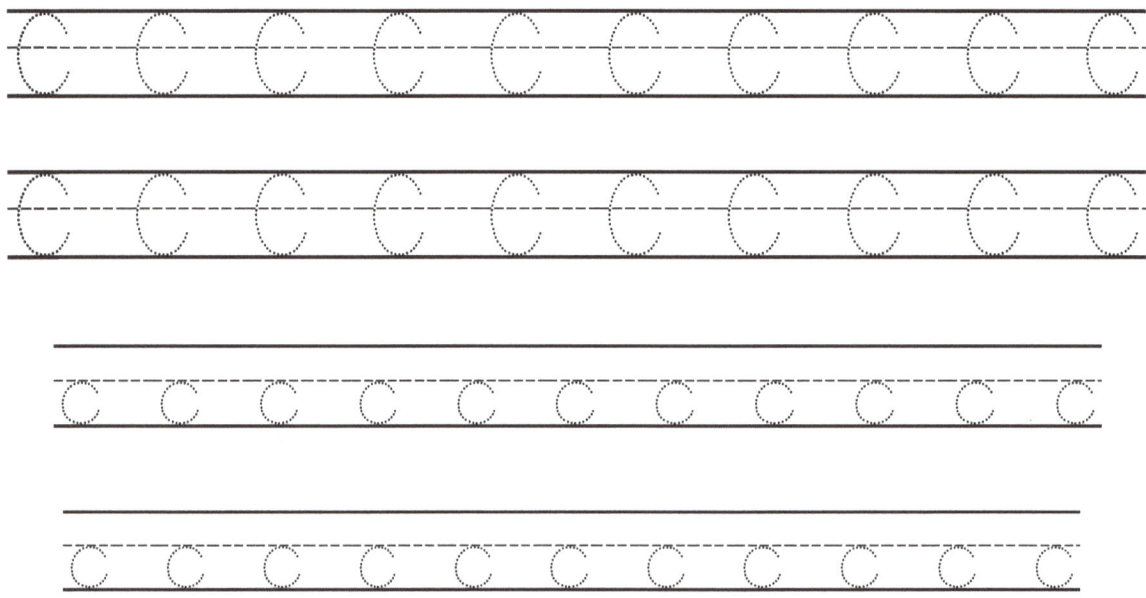

C sounds like /s/ when it comes before:

e, i, or y

Draw a line to match the picture with the first sound

Color 3 pictures with the ČČ sound in blue.

Sound and blend.

fāce   rāce   lāce   pāce   čĕll   čĕnt
čīte   mīce   nīce   rīce   līce   cēase

Read, trace and copy.

face   race   lace

pace   cell   cent

cite   mice   nice

rice   lice   cease

Trace the letters.

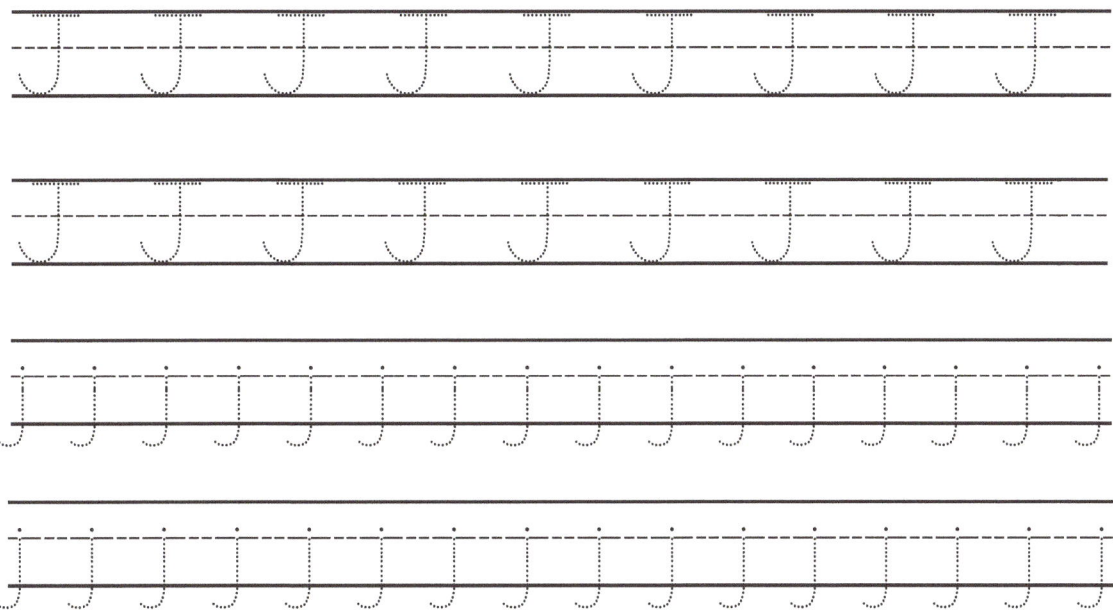

Draw a line to match the picture with the first sound

Color 4 pictures with the Jj sound in pink.

Sound and blend.

jär jăb jŏb jōke jerk

jĕt jăm jĕst

Read, trace and copy.

jar   jab

job   joke

jerk   jet

jam   jest

Trace the letters.

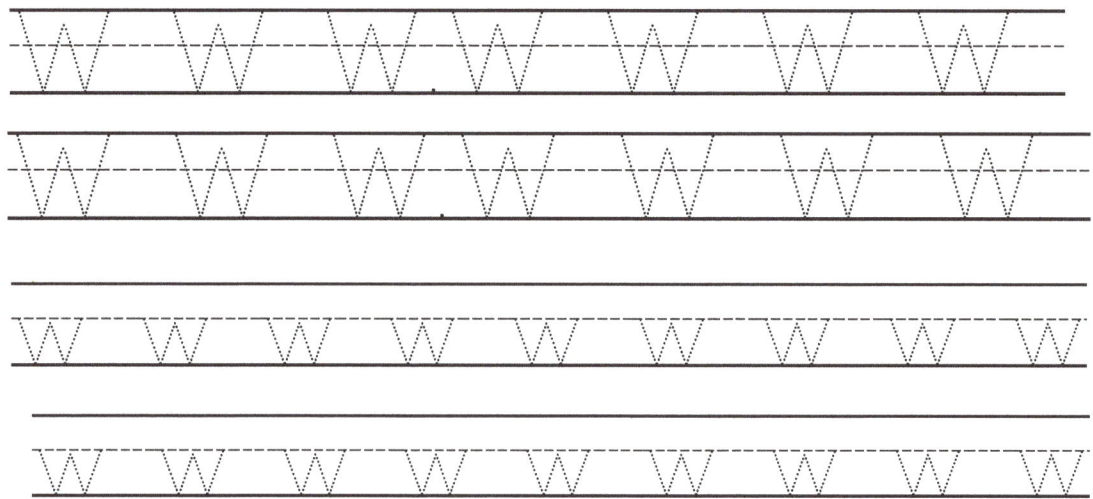

Draw a line to match the picture with the first sound.

98

Color 4 pictures with the Ww sound in blue.

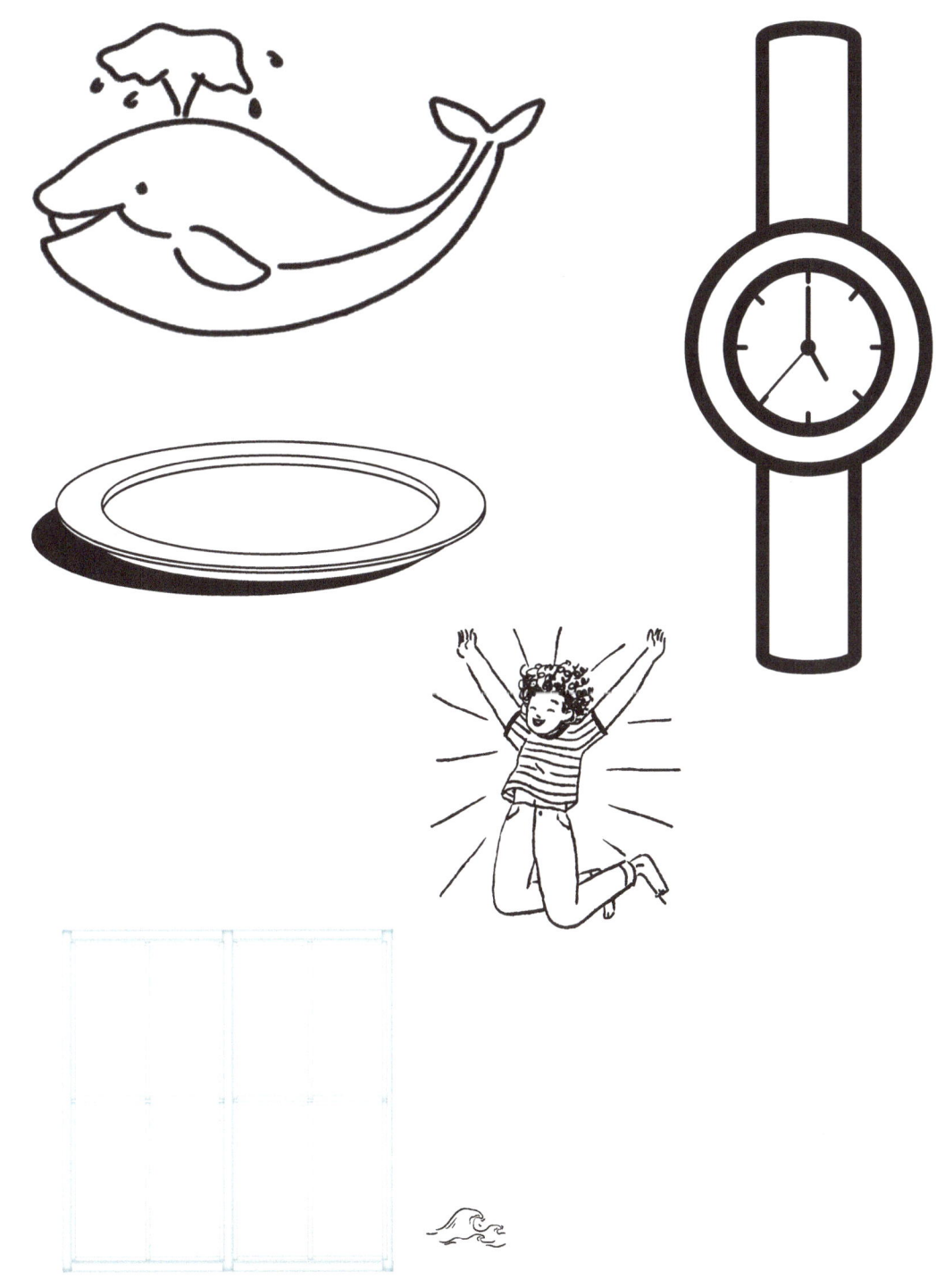

Sound and blend.

wĕb wĕt wĕpt wĕst wĕll wĕnt
wīde wīpe wīfe wīse wĭn wĭll

Read, trace and copy.

web   wet   wept

west   well   went

wide   wipe   wife

wise   win   will

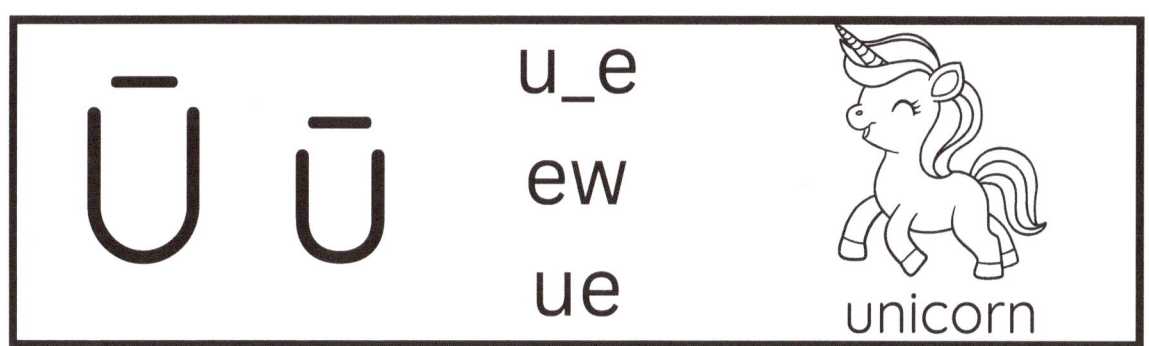

Trace the letters.

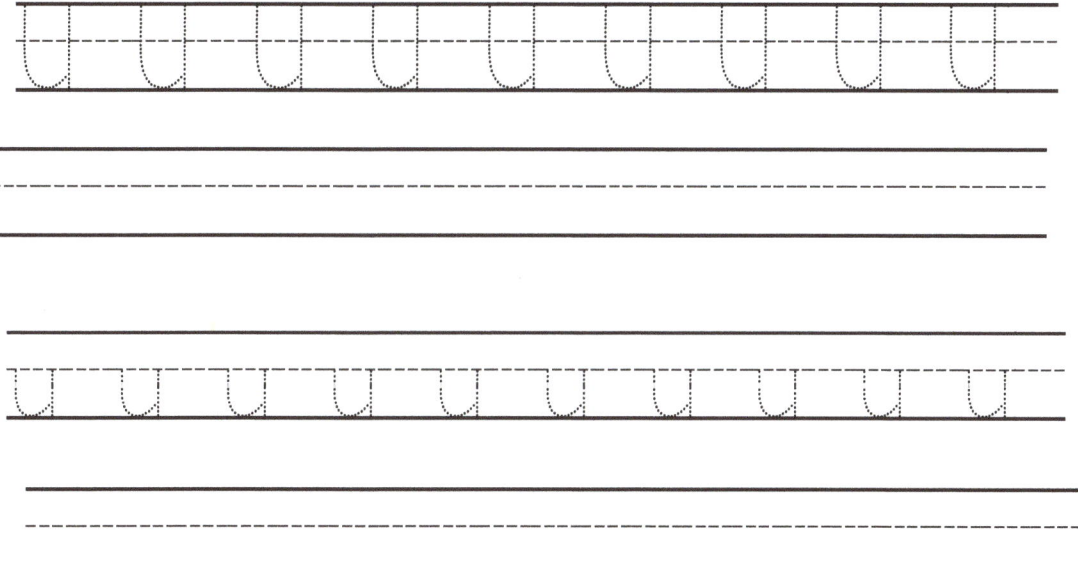

The "e" is silent and makes the "u" say its name.

If ew comes after d, n, s, or t – it usually says /yoo/ (like "new").

After l, r, or s – say /oo/ (like "blue"); after t or q – say /yoo/ (like "rescue").

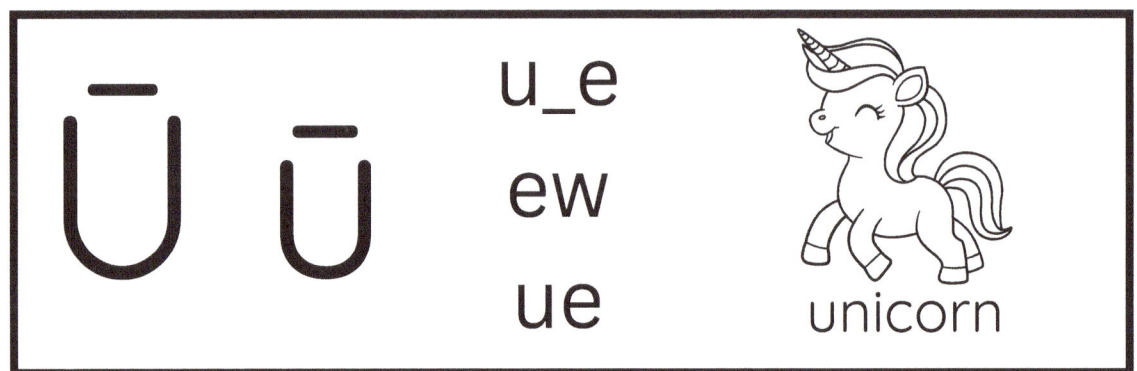

Trace the letters.

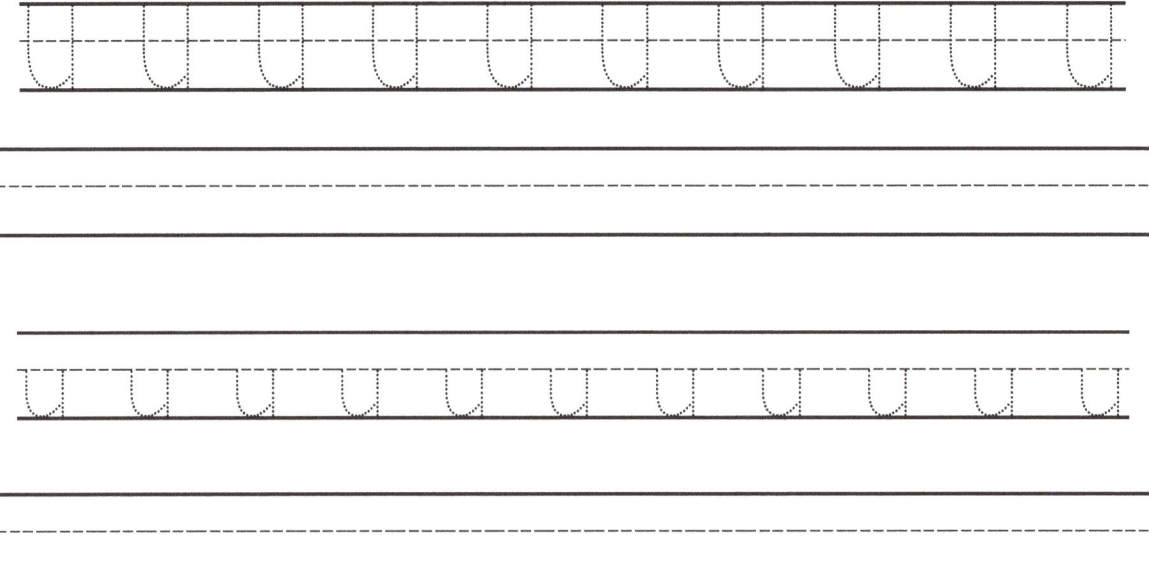

The "e" is silent and makes the "u" say its name.

If ew comes after d, n, s, or t – it usually says /yoo/ (like "new").

After l, r, or s – say /oo/ (like "blue"); after t or q – say /yoo/ (like "rescue").

Color 3 pictures with the Ūū sound in pink.

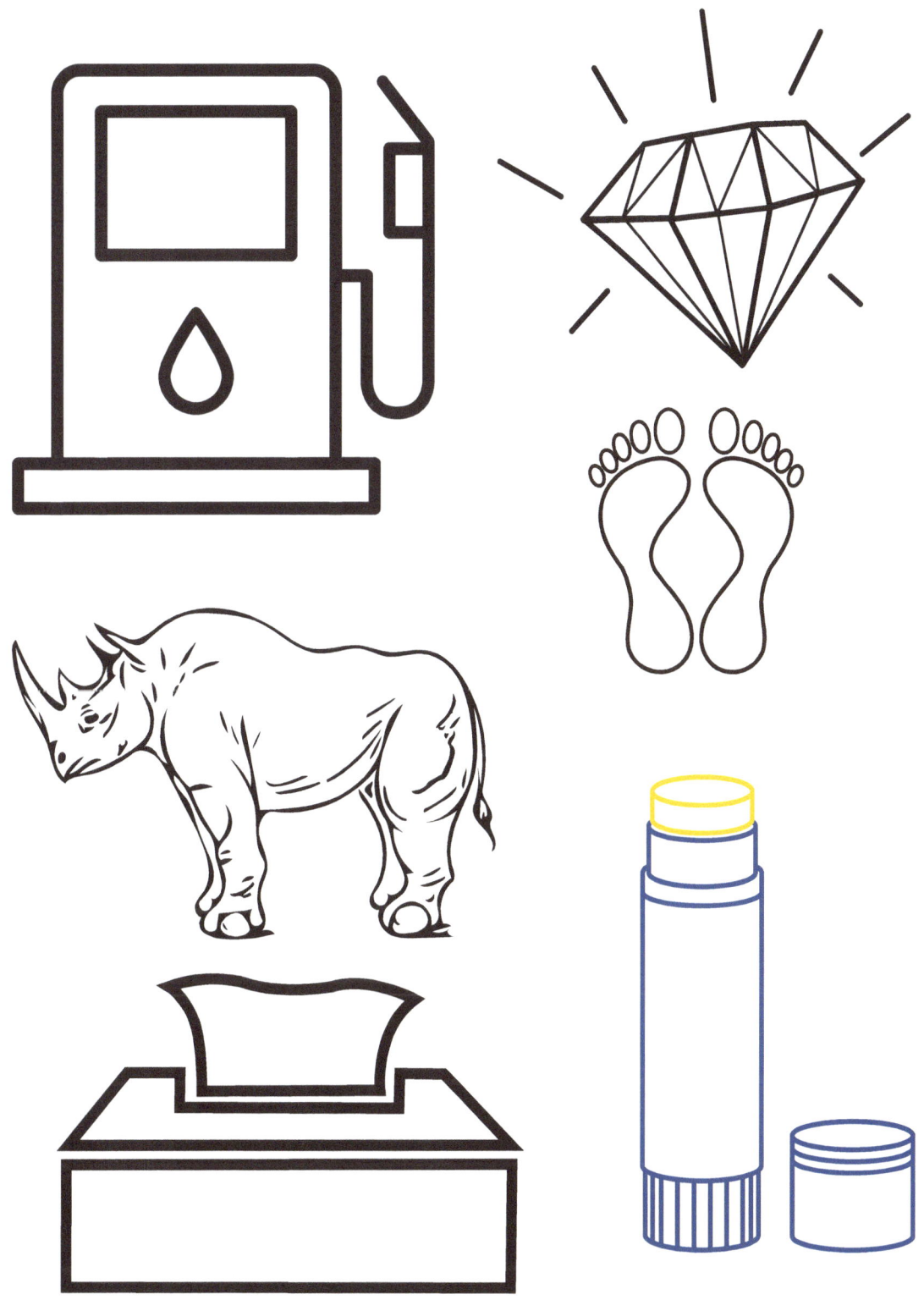

Sound and blend.

mūle cūte cūbe tūbe mūte tūne
vacūūm dūke jūice dūne ūse fūse

Read, trace and copy.

mule　　　　　cute　　　　　cube

tube　　　　　mute　　　　　tune

vacuum　　　　duke　　　　　juice

use　　　　　dune　　　　　fuse

Trace the letters.

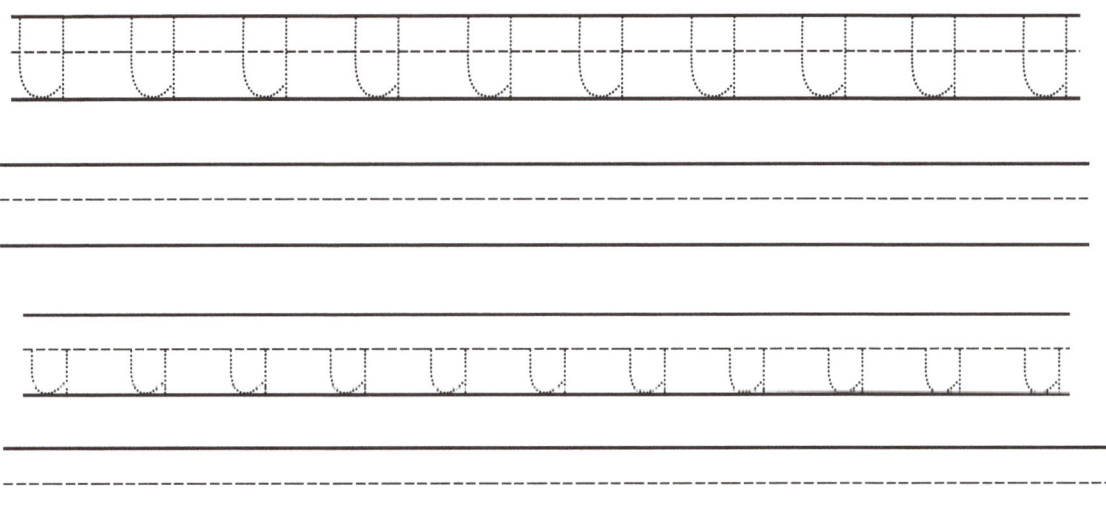

Draw a line to match these pictures.

Color 4 pictures with the Ŭŭ sound in yellow.

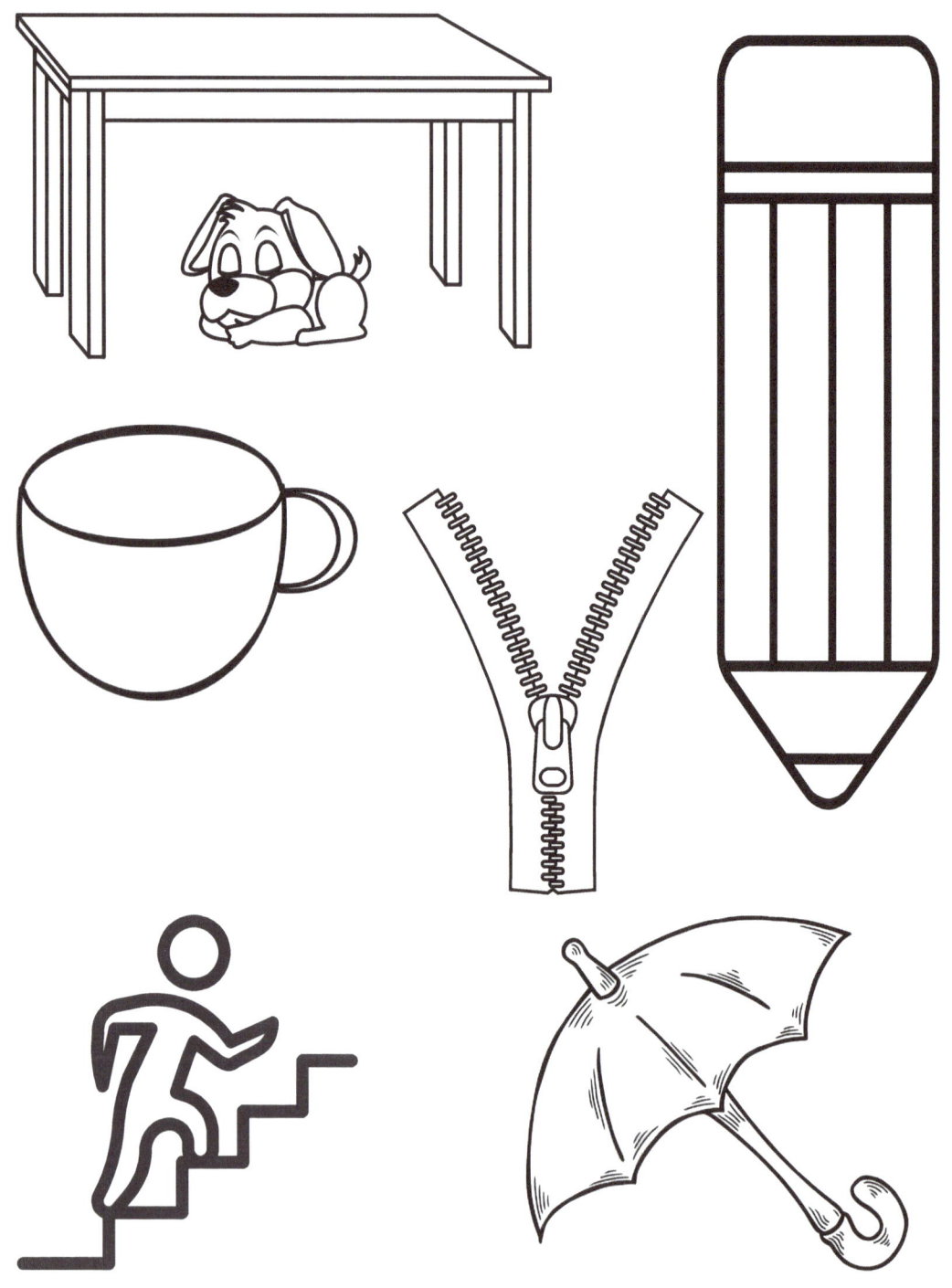

Sound and blend.

cūb tŭb hŭb rŭb pŭp cūp
cūd bŭd mŭd fŭss bŭs sŭn

Read, trace and copy.

cub tub hub

rub pup cup

cud bud mud

fuss bus sun

Sound and blend.

sŭm hŭm fŭn rŭn jŭnk bŭnk
sŭnk mŭst trŭst rŭst bŭst dŭck

Read, trace and copy.

sum　　　　　　hum　　　　　　fun

run　　　　　　junk　　　　　　bunk

sunk　　　　　　must　　　　　　trust

rust　　　　　　bust　　　　　　duck

Sound and blend.

cūt nŭt hŭt bŭt rŭg bŭg
hŭg dŭg gŭn gŭm gŭst gŭt

Read, trace and copy.

cut   nut   hut

but   rug   bug

hug   dug   gun

gum   gust   gut

V v

vulture

Trace the letters.

V V V V V V V V V

V V V V V V V V V

v v v v v v v v v v v

v v v v v v v v v v v

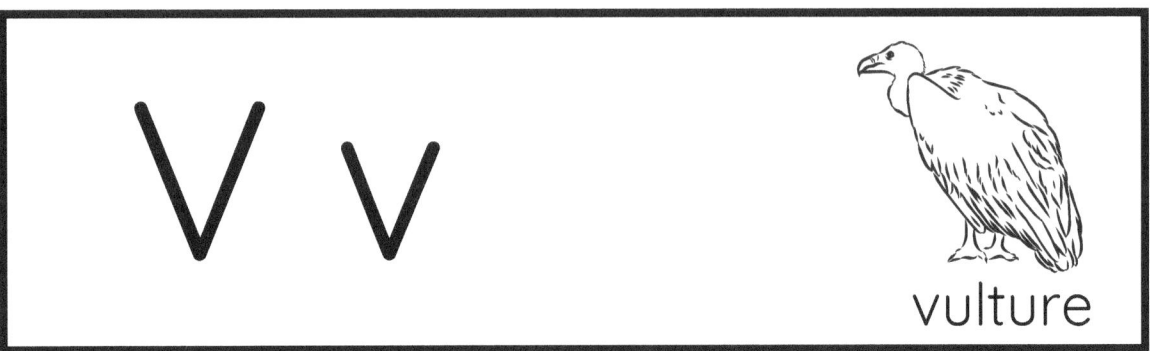

Color 4 pictures with the Vv sound in purple.

Sound and blend.

ğāve cāve pāve sāve wāve slāve

brāve crāve ğrāve vāle vāse vāin

Read, trace and copy.

gave   cave   pave

save   wave   slave

brave   crave   grave

vake   vase   vain

Sound and blend.

hăve vălley lēave wēave hēave věst

līve dīve hīve wīves vīne vīce

Read, trace and copy.

have   valley

leave   weave   heave

vest   live   dive

wives   vine   vice

Sound and blend.

vīle cōve dōve wōve rōve ğrōve

Read, trace and copy.

vile   cove

dove   wove

rove   grove

English words do not end in:
i, u, v, j

Trace the letters.

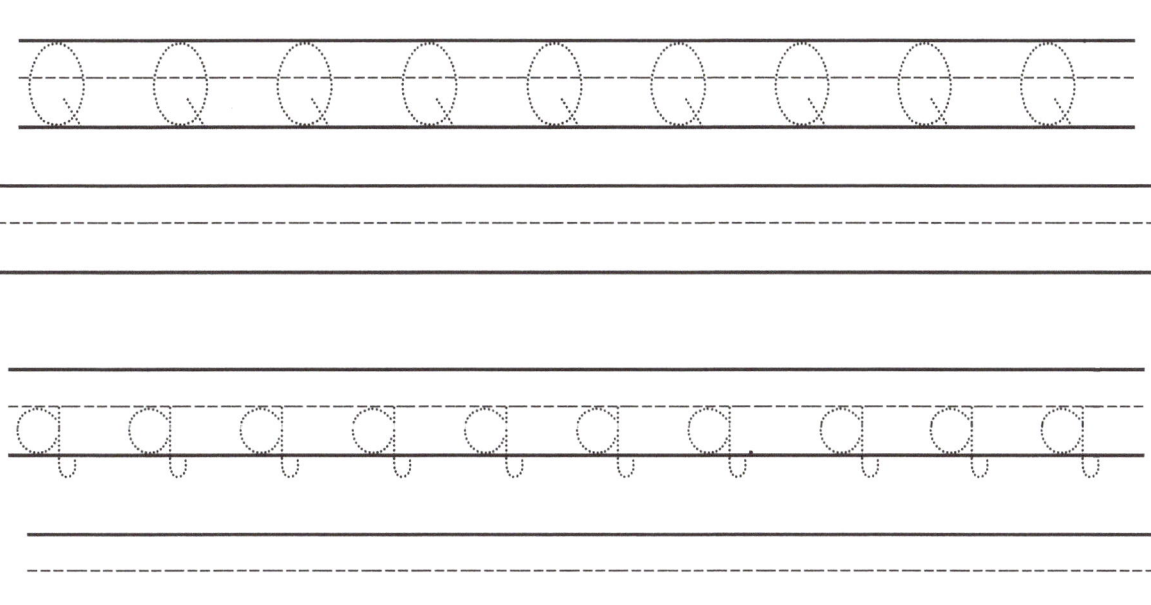

Draw a line to match these pictures.

Circle 3 pictures with the Qq sound.

Sound and blend.

Qq always goes with u, it always starts with qu

quāke quāil quăck quēēn quĭck quŏte
quĕll quīte quĭt quĭp quĭlt quĭck

Read, trace and copy.

quake quail quack

queen quick quote

quell quite quit

quip quilt quick

xenops

Trace the letters.

/ks/ (the most common sound) box, next
/z/ in a few words (especially Greek origin) xylophone, Xavier
/gz/ (like "g + z") when it comes between vowels/ksh/ in some longer words (Latin origin) anxious, luxury

Circle 5 pictures with the Xx sound.

Sound and blend.

ŏx fŏx bŏx ăxe tăx wăx

vĕx mĭx fĭx tŭx

Read, trace and copy.

ox					fox

box					axe

tax			wax			vex

mix			fix			tux

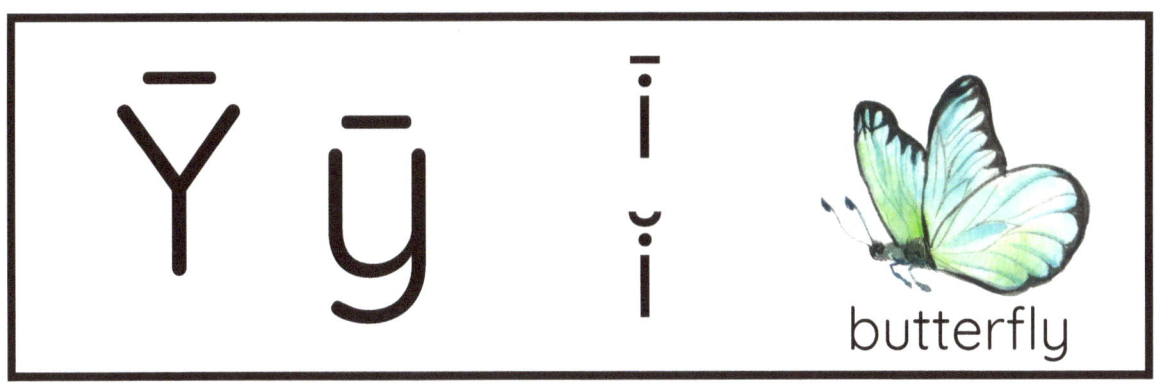

Trace the letters.

End of short words e.g cry, my Middle of a word e.g myth, gym End of long words e.g happy, candy

Circle 3 pictures with the Ȳ ȳ sound.

Sound and blend.

bȳe rȳe lȳe bȳ skȳ mȳ c̄rȳ

spȳ flȳ plȳ slȳ drȳ frȳ prȳ

Read, trace and copy.

bye   rye   lye

by   sky   my

cry   spy   fly

ply   sly   dry

fry   pry

Trace the letters.

Circle 4 pictures with the Ў ў sound.

125

Sound and blend.

y̆ăm y̆ăp y̆ĕar y̆ard y̆arn y̆awn

y̆awl y̆acht y̆ēast y̆ĕt y̆ŭm

Read, trace and copy.

yam   yap   year

yard   yarn   yawn

yawl   yacht   yeast

yet   yum

Sound and blend.

yĕll yiēld yoū yoūr yūle
yōlk yōke yŏre yĕlp yĕs

Read, trace and copy.

yell   yield   you

your   yule   yolk

yoke   yore

yelp   yes

Z z

zebra

Trace the letters.

Circle 4 pictures with the Zz sound.

Sound and blend.

zăx zàrf zĕst zĭp
zĭnk zŏne zēal zērŏ

Read, trace and copy.

zax   zarf

zest   zip

zink   zone

zero   zeal

CERTIFICATE OF COMPLETION

is awarded to

_____

for successfully completing

Phonics & Blending Book 1

- Long vowel sounds
- Short vowel sounds
- Blending sounds
- Handwriting
- Letter recognition
- Some spelling rules

_____
Date

_____
Signature

MBONENI FOUNDATION

www.ingramcontent.com/pod-product-compliance
Lightning Source LLC
Chambersburg PA
CBHW041550220426
43666CB00002B/23